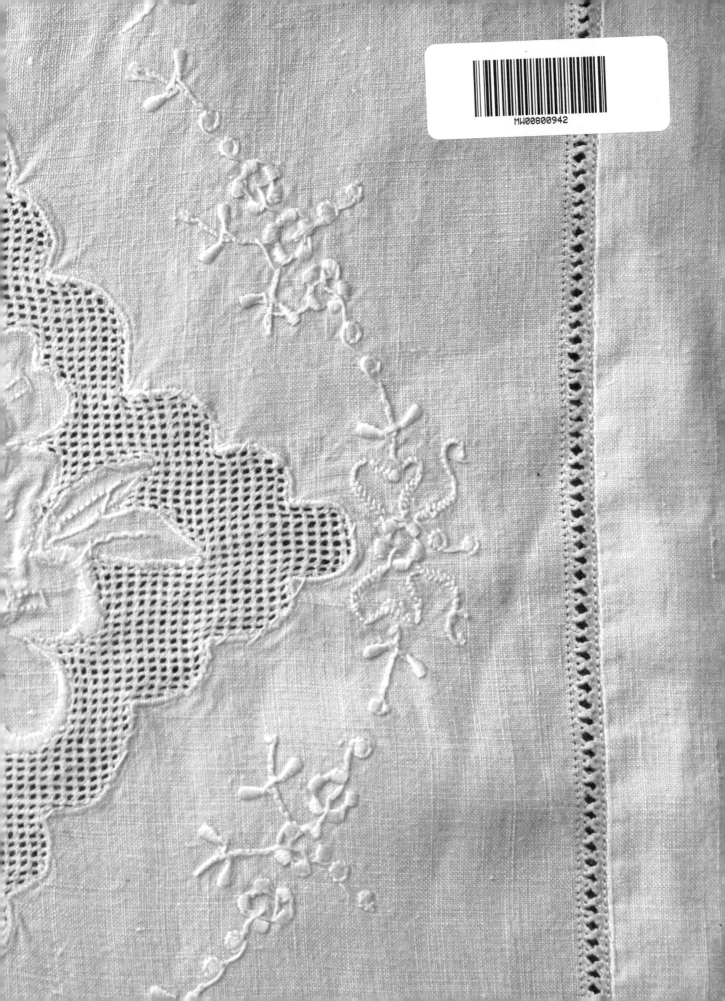

The Italian Daughter's Cookbook

This book is dedicated to my husband Joe
and children, Alessandra, Domenico, and Isabella.
You are my world.

In loving memory of my parents,
Domenico and Maria Coluccio.

"A Casa Si Mangia Bene."

At Home You Eat Well.

The Italian Daughter's Cookbook

By Cathy Coluccio Fazzolari

Photographed by Daniel Paterna

pH powerHouse Books   Brooklyn New York

My memories of the crackling sound of zeppole being kneaded, the aroma of Sunday sauce permeating my childhood home, and the burst of hot air that hit my face when foil was lifted from baked lamb inspired me to write this book. I wanted to capture my mother's recipes, none of which were written down. Using my senses of taste and smell, as well as touch and hearing, I recreated the dishes I remember from my childhood.

The hardest part of putting the recipes into writing was determining the measurements. When I cooked with my mother, we judged the amount with our eyes, using the palm of our hands as a measuring spoon. To a large pot of water, we added a full palm of salt, to a smaller one, half of a palm's worth. In formulating these recipes, my daughter Isabella was my assistant, measuring and recording the amount of every ingredient before I added it to a dish.

In my mother's kitchen, we used few tools of any kind. We never sliced on a cutting board. Vegetables were cut above the pot, using our thumbs to release the slices into the pot. The smell of foods (like a well-browned roast) or their appearance (like the oil on the surface of tomato sauce) served as our timer. To purée tomatoes, we squished them with our hands in a colander. I learned to peel potatoes with a paring knife, rather than a vegetable peeler. Today, I still rely on the pad of my thumb to help me cut, but I now often use an electronic timer, a hand-cranked vegetable mill, and a swivel peeler. And I confess that I sometimes use an instant-read thermometer to judge the internal temperature of roasts, especially when I want to serve them rare.

When I was a teenager, my mother began buying me dishes, glassware, and pots and pans which were sold to her by Antonio Pantusa, a Cook-O-Matic salesman, which she paid for in installments over a three-year period. In New York, it was common for Italian immigrants to purchase housewares in this manner. My mother felt it was her obligation to make sure I was well equipped to begin my married life. I still use many of the pots and pans that she gifted me. It was also important to her to set the table with a tablecloth every night. She had a large assortment of cloths that she bought when she visited Italy. I am now the proud owner of her collection and used many of the tablecloths featured throughout this book.

My Family Story

My parents and five siblings were born in Marina di Gioiosa Ionica, a small coastal town in Reggio Calabria, one of the five provinces of Calabria in Southern Italy. My father, Domenico Coluccio, and oldest brother, Luigi, immigrated to America in the late 1950s in search of a better life for the family. They settled in Brooklyn, New York. In 1964, they decided it was time for my mother and the rest of the children to join them in America. Soon after, my father founded the legendary Italian specialty store known as D. Coluccio & Sons, along with my brothers, Luigi and Rocco. Today, I am a co-owner with my brothers of the family business. We import and distribute Italian specialty products from all parts of Italy—with an emphasis on those from Calabria—and operate a retail shop next door to the wholesale location.

As the youngest of six children, I was the first in my family to be born in America. As far back as I can remember, my parents introduced me as "questa e' l'Americana," meaning "this is the American." I grew up in the store and was constantly by my father's side. Some of my earliest childhood memories took place right there in that store: ringing up at the cash register at five years old, buttering rolls at seven, and making sandwiches at ten. My family lived upstairs from the shop and I walked through it to get in and out of our apartment. The store's rhythms were as familiar to me as the daily routines of my home life. If my mother was cooking dinner and suddenly found she was missing an ingredient, I ran downstairs to get it, rummaging through the store shelves as casually as if they were our pantry.

Growing up, I thought that all of Italy must have immigrated to Brooklyn. When someone asked an Italian immigrant where they were from, the answer would be Naples, Calabria, Rome, or Sicily. My first spoken language was the Calabrese dialect, and English my second. I only needed to speak a few words of dialect to be perceived as fellow Calabrese and not just as "the American."

When it first opened on 59th Street in Borough Park, Brooklyn, Coluccio's was a typical neighborhood corner store. It sold coffee and buttered rolls in the morning, as well as staples like milk and eggs. My father noted the abundance of Italian immigrants in Brooklyn but the lack of ingredients from their homeland. He saw the potential to become a successful importer and the business was built on his vision. His first offering was the signature olive from his village in Calabria. These tiny green "Calabrese" olives, cured in a brine of garlic, salt, fennel, and hot peppers, were unheard of in America at that time. Along with other imports—Soresina provolone cheese, canned Italian tomatoes, Calabrian chili peppers, and Italian dried pastas—these items brought a regular parade of Italian American customers into Coluccio's and the numbers increased with each passing year.

Salumerias and pork stores began popping up and serving Italian American communities all over cities in the United States with large Italian immigrant populations. Coluccio's began selling to many of these small businesses. By 1974, our location was unable to accommodate the growing wholesale orders. We purchased a much larger space. My family moved into the house next door but continued to operate the original corner grocery store on 59th Street. Today, we are on 60th Street between 12th and 13th Avenues in Brooklyn.

Around 1978, my father had the brilliant idea of closing the grocery and creating an Italian specialty emporium. We combined the wholesale showroom with a retail store, allowing clients to come and see the food in person as well as to feel the excitement of in-store shopping. It was a prescient move, since Italy and Italian products became of nation-wide interest in the 1980s. Sun-dried tomatoes and Calabrian chili peppers, two products which my father was the first to import, became staples in many Italian-American households. In a short time, we began to distribute not only to Italian specialty stores, but also to other distributors and importers around the country. Our regular clientele started to include customers from a variety of cultural backgrounds. On June 15, 2010, my father was posthumously inducted into the Italian Trade Commission's "Hall of Fame" for his work and efforts in bringing Italian foods to America.

While many in the business know me as the daughter of Domenico Coluccio, those who have seen and tasted my cooking recognize me as the daughter of my mother, Maria "Maruzza" Coluccio. She was a matriarch who cooked delicious meals and maintained Calabrese

traditions in New York. Every night, she provided multi-course homemade dinners. We often had unexpected guests and she could whip up exquisite meals in seemingly seconds without advance notice.

Born twenty-two years after my oldest brother, I was the youngest of the six children in my family. Since I was the last daughter living at home, I was often enlisted to help prepare the meals, becoming my mother's sous chef at the age of four. I washed parsley, chopped onions, peeled garlic, puréed tomatoes, and prepped any other ingredients needed for dinner. After helping her prep, I set the table while she cooked the meal. Being raised by a mother who was born in Italy in the 1920s was not typical for someone of my generation nor were the lessons I was taught. She would always say: "Watch me. One day you will be doing this in your own home" or "When I am not here you will always remember my teaching." While my father showed me how to succeed in business, my mother taught me to excel in cooking.

One of the secrets to the constant stream of elaborate meals that my mother created was her fully stocked pantry of homemade delicacies. Always on her kitchen shelves were sliced eggplants packed in a clay pot, jars of peppers stuffed with anchovies and capers, and dried peppers hanging from a string. Every February, we made soppressata, dried sausage, and capicola and consumed them for months afterward. I remember assisting with the making of the salami on many cold winter days. My job was to tie the links—an important responsibility because if the string was too tight, the casing could break, and if it was too loose, air could get in and spoil the salami. My parents taught me how to cure and store the sausages safely so we could enjoy them for the rest of the year.

After years of cooking alongside my mother, I not only mastered a variety of recipes but also picked up the tricks she used in the kitchen. Like Calabrese mothers had been teaching their daughters to cook for generations, I learned the traditions of my ancestors as well as my mother. One tip I learned is that a tea kettle can save any dish. Hot water helps if there's not enough water in the pasta pot, too much salt in a dish, pasta and vegetable dishes are too

starchy, a cacciatore is too dry, or you need to create gravy for a roast. My mother showed me that a drizzle of extra virgin olive oil and a dusting of freshly grated Parmigiano cheese can make last night's leftovers taste like they were just cooked. I was taught to roll fresh pasta around a knitting needle to create irregular shapes so that sauce clings in a way it can't to commercial dried pasta. In my family, Christmas was celebrated with fig cookies made with vincotto. My mother kept family traditions alive with her devotion to the Calabrese way. I have passed them on to my children with the hope they will pass them on to theirs.

In 1991, I reinforced my Calabrese roots when I married Joseph Fazzolari, a Calabrese immigrant who came to America when he was three years old. I was blessed to then learn

from another great cook, my mother-in-law, Esterina Fazzolari. She made all the Calabrese specialties, including homemade olives, spicy pancetta, and soppressata. Throughout my years of marriage, I have replicated the many dishes of both my mother and my mother-in-law. One of the two greatest compliments I have ever received was from my husband who said, "I think I like your sauce better than my mother's." The other was from my mother, who remarked, "This lasagna tastes just like mine."

Joseph and I have three beautiful children: Alessandra, Domenico, and Isabella. They share my passion for Italian cooking and are blessed to have had the influence of both of their grandmothers in their lives. One day, while we were making lasagna together, Alessandra reminded me, "Nonna always put an egg in her ricotta." When we began shaping the meatballs, Isabella remembered, "Nanni always dipped her fingers in olive oil before she began rolling the meatballs." I love how closely my children watched their grandmothers and me while we cooked. It's the way that cooking has been passed down in our family for years, and it's gratifying to see the custom continuing into the next generation. Many dishes from my heritage were not written down because the Calabrese assumed that a daughter would know all her mother's recipes. A mother always made sure her daughter knew how to cook, because a young woman with no cooking skills was a poor reflection on the family and would have trouble finding a husband. While times have certainly changed, the importance of learning to cook has not disappeared. I continue to pass these traditions on to my three children not with the intention of making them more eligible for marriage, but to teach them the importance of healthy and sustainable diets as well as caring for themselves.

In *The Italian Daughter's Cookbook*, you will find the recipes that I have learned from my mother and mother-in-law and have passed down to my own children. These are the dishes I have cooked and eaten with my family for my entire life. While most of these dishes are Italian at heart, many of them are uniquely Calabrese and embody a regional style of cooking.

What Is Calabrese Food?

Calabrese cooking is very different from the Italian cooking we read about and watch on television. You'll recognize the Italian sensibility that you love but notice a difference in ingredients and techniques. Butter, cream, and stocks are rarely used. Many of the recipes require just a few items and a couple of steps. To cook authentic Calabrese food, it is essential to use fresh, high-quality products. While there is a widely held misconception that Calabrese cooking consists solely of spicy foods, the reality is that it yields healthy dishes, in which no single ingredient overpowers the others. It will take you less time than usual to prepare the Calabrese version of Sunday sauce with meatballs and you'll be rewarded with an incomparably lighter dish. You'll love the Calabrese one-pot technique for turning fresh vegetables, legumes, and pasta into delicious, healthy, and unmistakably Italian meals. Leafy greens, dried and fresh beans, olives, olive oils, eggs, and lean meats are integral to Southern Italy.

My parents and me in Italy

18

Vegetable

Eggplant "Meatballs"

Yields about 9 "meatballs"

- 1 large eggplant or 2 medium about 2 lbs
- 1 tablespoon sea salt for boiling
- 1 large egg
- 6 basil leaves finely chopped
- 3 garlic cloves minced

handwritten: Fried Eggplant Meatballs

TABLE OF CONTENTS

Antipasto

Arancini
Rice Balls

Cavolfiori Fritti
Fried Cauliflower

Carciofi Ripieni
Stuffed Artichokes

Funghi Ripieni
Stuffed Mushrooms

Melanzane Ripiene
Stuffed Eggplant

Crocchette di Patate
Potato Croquettes

Frittelle di Fiore di Zucchine
Zucchini Flower Fritters

Funghi Porcini Fritti
Fried Porcini Mushrooms

Insalata di Mare
Seafood Salad

Prosciutto con Melone
Proscuitto with Melon

Polpo alla Griglia
Grilled Octopus

Antipasto di Formaggio Assortito, Soppressata e Verdure Sott'aceto
Antipasto of Assorted Cheeses, Soppressata, and Pickled Vegetables

Traditional Italian dinners consist of three piattos: antipasto (before the meal), primo (pasta), and secondo (meat or fish), followed by salad, fruit, and coffee. In America, antipasto would be considered the appetizers. In my mother's kitchen, antipasti were served while the pasta was being cooked and the meat or main dish was being prepared. Often, my mother and I would eat the antipasto while the pasta was boiling. We were not used to sitting down at the table with the rest of the family.

Antipasti were usually prepared from ingredients that were readily available in our pantry and refrigerator. In the summer, fresh vegetables that were abundant in our backyard were included. In the winter, we'd put out jarred or pickled items. The occasion and the guest list dictated the extent of the antipasti. The array always included an assortment of cheeses, homemade salamis, and bread, all of which were never pre-sliced but expertly cut just before they were set out. Olives were also a constant and usually zucchini flower fritters or stuffed eggplant, our family's favorite, as well. For birthdays or holidays, the assortment of antipasto could be expansive.

Many of the items, especially in the summer, were fried vegetables. Pure olive oil was always used for frying because it has a higher smoke point than other olive oils. Extra virgin olive oil was used as a topping or for sautéing. To get perfect results, it's important to use a generous amount of oil and heat it to the specified temperature before adding the food. Contrary to popular belief, food that is cooked in a larger quantity of oil will absorb less oil and be less greasy than that cooked in a small amount.

After frying, we collected all of the oil in a large white tub. When the tub was full, we added lye to the oil to turn it into laundry soap. To this day, I remember the clean scent of my clothes that were washed with it. Whites came out pristine, as if they were brand new. It is the Calabrese way to let nothing go to waste.

Makes about 3 dozen

2 teaspoons sea salt

3 ounces prosciutto di Parma, finely chopped

4 cups Arborio rice (2 pounds)

1½ cups freshly grated cheese (Parmigiano Reggiano or Grana Padano)

1½ teaspoons freshly ground black pepper

7 large eggs

1½ pounds whole milk ricotta, drained

½ pound mozzarella cheese, shredded

2½ cups breadcrumbs

10 cups pure olive oil, for frying

Arancini
Rice Balls

In my opinion, there is nothing more delicious than freshly fried rice balls from Faicco's Pork Store. My family is always so excited when I bring them home. This is my version of the cheesy and creamy fried appetizer.

In a large pot, bring 3 quarts of water to a boil. Add salt and prosciutto, then slowly add the rice, stirring continuously. Bring again to a boil, reduce heat to medium-low and cook semi-covered, stirring occasionally for 16 to 18 minutes or until the rice is tender.

Remove from heat and add the grated cheese and pepper. Mix well and let sit uncovered for about 5 minutes.

Spread the rice in a large baking dish and let cool for about 1 hour.

In a separate bowl, combine 3 eggs and ricotta. Add to the rice mixture, then add the mozzarella, and mix well.

Using an ice cream scooper, scoop out a heaping amount of the mixture and roll tight with your palms to make the perfect round ball. Place on a baking sheet lined with parchment paper. Refrigerate for at least 4 hours or overnight.

In a separate bowl, beat the 4 remaining eggs. Dip the rice balls in the beaten eggs, then roll in the breadcrumbs, and place on a cookie sheet. Continue until all rice balls are coated.

In a 6-quart pot, heat oil (about 2 inches in depth) to a temperature of 350°F. Add a few rice balls at a time, making sure not to overcrowd the pot. Reduce heat slightly and continue frying until they are golden brown in color. Remove each with a slotted spoon and place on a paper towel to absorb excess oil. Repeat with the remaining rice balls.

Let sit for about 30 minutes. Serve at room temperature.

Note: Rice balls can be frozen for up to 2 weeks after they are fried. Defrost overnight in the refrigerator and reheat in the oven on a parchment-lined baking sheet at 375°F for about 20 minutes.

Serves 4–6

1 head cauliflower

1 tablespoon sea salt

3 large eggs

2 tablespoons freshly grated cheese (Parmigiano Reggiano, Grana Padano, or Pecorino Romano), plus more for serving

1½ cups breadcrumbs

4 cups pure olive oil, for frying

Cavolfiori Fritti

Fried Cauliflower

Cauliflower is part of the cruciferous vegetable family and has many known health benefits. Since it is available year-round, this appetizer can be made anytime. It is very simple to make and can be prepared hours ahead of time and served at room temperature.

Remove and discard stem and outer leaves of the cauliflower, then cut in half. Remove and discard any additional stem. Cut in half again and separate the florets. You should have about 5 pieces from each half. Wash and rinse well.

Place 8 cups of cold water, cauliflower, and salt in a 6-quart pot. Bring to a boil, reduce heat to medium, and continue to cook for 2 minutes.

Gently remove cauliflower with a slotted spoon and place in a colander. Let cool.

Mix together eggs and cheese. Dip the cooled cauliflower florets in the egg mixture and then in the breadcrumbs.

In a 13-inch frying pan over medium-high heat, add the oil (about ½-inch in depth) and heat for 3 to 4 minutes. To test the oil, place a pinch of the cauliflower coating in the oil; if it begins to sizzle, the oil is ready. Add the breaded cauliflower in a single layer, reduce heat slightly, and fry until golden brown on all sides. Remove from the pan and place on a paper towel to absorb excess oil.

Serve warm or at room temperature with additional freshly grated cheese.

Serves 4

1 cup breadcrumbs

½ cup freshly grated cheese (Parmigiano Reggiano, Grana Padano, or Pecorino Romano)

½ cup fresh parsley, finely chopped

2 garlic cloves, minced

6 tablespoons extra virgin olive oil

4 large fresh artichokes

1 lemon, cut in quarters

1 teaspoon sea salt

Sewing thread, optional

Carciofi Ripieni
Stuffed Artichokes

Stuffed artichokes are usually served as an appetizer in the spring months during their peak season. Always look for dark green artichokes with leaves that are tightly packed. Adding lemon wedges while the artichokes boil will help prevent them from turning brown.

To prepare the stuffing mixture, mix the breadcrumbs, cheese, parsley, garlic, and 2 tablespoons oil in a bowl. Set aside.

To wash the artichokes, remove and discard about 1 inch of the stem. Peel the outside of the remaining stem. Remove and discard outer leaves. Cut and discard about 1 inch of the top portion of the artichokes (removing the hard needles). Rinse in cold water.

In a large pot with 3 quarts of cold water, add artichokes, lemon, and salt and bring to a boil. Continue cooking for 4 to 5 minutes, then immediately remove the artichokes. Place in a colander and set aside.

When cool, gently open the leaves of the artichokes and stuff each layer of leaves with the stuffing mixture. If using sewing thread, wrap around the artichoke and knot tightly to prevent the stuffing from falling out.

In a large pot that can fit the artichokes in one layer, bring to a boil 1½ cups of water and remaining 4 tablespoons of oil. Add stuffed artichokes, reduce heat to medium-low, and cook covered for about 30 minutes. Rotate the artichokes occasionally.

Remove the artichokes from the pot. If used sewing thread, remove and discard the thread. Place artichokes on a serving platter, and top with the juices from the bottom of the pot.

Serve warm.

Makes 2 dozen

1 pound white button mushrooms

1 teaspoon sea salt

1 cup breadcrumbs

5 sprigs fresh parsley, finely chopped

1 cup freshly grated cheese (Parmigiano Reggiano, Grana Padano, or Pecorino Romano)

3 garlic cloves, minced

1 cup whole milk

10 tablespoons pure olive oil

⅛ teaspoon freshly ground black pepper

Funghi Ripieni
Stuffed Mushrooms

What would Thanksgiving dinner be without stuffed mushrooms? This recipe is my mother-in-law's and is very unique. There are no ground meat or eggs added to the stuffing. Instead, the stuffing is bound by milk. Be sure to look for bright white button mushrooms with no brown spots. Larger mushrooms can usually be found in the weeks leading up to Thanksgiving in oblong wooden crates.

Rinse each mushroom gently under cold water, pat dry with a paper towel, and remove the stems entirely.

Place the mushroom tops in a dish, sprinkle with ¼ teaspoon salt, and set aside.

Place the mushroom stems in a saucepan with ½ teaspoon salt and ½ cup of water and bring to a boil. Continue boiling for about 3 minutes. Drain in colander and then cut the stems into small pieces.

Preheat the oven to 375°F.

In a large bowl, place the stems, breadcrumbs, parsley, cheese, garlic, ¼ teaspoon salt, 2 tablespoons oil, and pepper. Mix well. Add the milk and continue to mix until you have a paste-like mixture.

With your hands, tightly pack each mushroom top with the stuffing. Set aside.

In a baking dish, place a very thin layer of oil (about ¼ cup).

Place ¼ cup oil in a small bowl. Brush the mushroom top and stuffing mixture with the oil and then place in the baking dish. The mushrooms should fit in a single layer comfortably.

Place in the oven and bake for 35 to 40 minutes. Remove from the oven and let sit for about 5 minutes. Transfer mushrooms to a paper towel-lined dish to absorb excess oil.

Serve at room temperature.

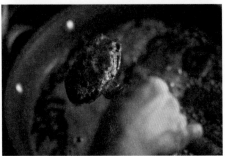

Makes 16 to 18

6 small eggplants (about 2½ pounds)

3¼ teaspoons sea salt

¾ cup breadcrumbs

¾ cup freshly grated cheese (Parmigiano Reggiano, Grana Padano, or Pecorino Romano), plus more for serving

3 large eggs

18 leaves fresh basil, chopped

3 garlic cloves, minced

⅛ teaspoon freshly ground black pepper

4 cups pure olive oil, for frying

Melanzane Ripiene
Stuffed Eggplant

Known by the Calabrese as "malangiani chini," this was my mother's signature dish. Anyone who has eaten at her home could attest to its deliciousness. If the eggplant skins break or you do not have enough skins, you can also stuff with cubanelle peppers (seeded, cored, and cut into quarters).

Wash eggplant, remove and discard stem, and then cut in half.

In a large pot with 6 cups of cold water, place eggplant and 1 tablespoon salt and bring to a boil. Continue cooking for about 18 minutes. Drain well in a colander and let cool.

Very gently remove the eggplant pulp from the skin, being sure not to tear the skin. Set aside the skin, which will be used as a shell for the stuffing mixture.

To prepare the stuffing, finely chop the eggplant pulp. In a bowl, combine the chopped eggplant, breadcrumbs, cheese, eggs, basil, garlic, ¼ teaspoon salt, and pepper. Mix well.

To stuff the eggplant skins, place the skin flat on your palm, take a heaping scoop of the mixture, and place on top of the skin. Use your other hand to press the mixture onto the skin until evenly spread throughout, smoothing the top and sides. Set aside.

In a 13-inch frying pan, add oil (about ½-inch in depth) and heat for 3 to 4 minutes on medium-high heat. To test the oil, place a pinch of the eggplant mixture in the oil; if it begins to sizzle, the oil is ready. Before placing the stuffed eggplant in the pan, use the remaining egg to make an egg wash and brush each one. Place the stuffed eggplant in batches, skin side up, in a single layer. Once golden brown, flip and cook the other side. Remove from the pan and place on a paper towel-lined dish to absorb excess oil.

Serve warm or at room temperature with additional freshly grated cheese.

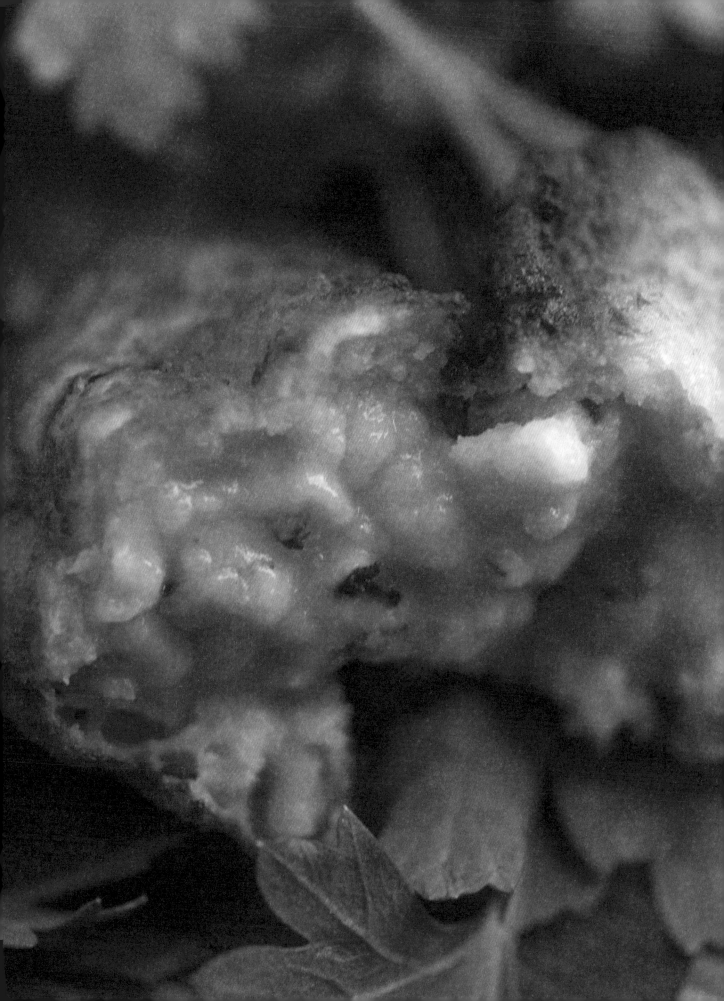

Makes 24 to 30

6 medium Yukon potatoes, boiled (see page 208)

½ tablespoon sea salt

1 cup freshly grated cheese (Parmigiana Reggiano or Grana Padano), plus more for serving

1 cup unbleached all-purpose flour, sifted

1 large egg

3 garlic cloves, minced

½ cup fresh basil, chopped

3¼ cup pure olive oil

Crocchette di Patate

Potato Croquettes

This is another one of my mother-in-law's signature appetizers. Whether she was serving them before a family dinner or as an after-school snack for my children, it was difficult to eat just one!

Prepare Boiled Potatoes according to recipe. Let cool and then peel the potatoes.

In a large bowl, mash the potatoes using a potato ricer or food mill. Add salt and mix well. Next, add the cheese, flour, egg, garlic, and basil. Mix until the ingredients are well combined.

Place about ¼ cup oil in a small bowl. To form the croquettes, dip your right-hand fingers into the oil, then line the palm of your left hand with the oil. Place a heaping tablespoon of the mixture into your oiled palm, form a log about 2 inches in length, and slightly pat down. Place on a dish and set aside. Repeat this step until all of the croquettes are formed.

In a 12-inch pan, add the remaining 3 cups of oil (about ½-inch in depth) and heat for 3 to 4 minutes on medium-high heat. To test the oil, place a pinch of the croquette mixture in the oil; if it begins to sizzle, the oil is ready. Reduce the heat slightly and begin adding the croquettes in a single layer. Fry until golden brown on all sides. Remove from the pan and place on a paper towel-lined dish to absorb excess oil.

Serve warm or at room temperature with additional freshly grated cheese.

Frittelle di Fiore di Zucchine

Zucchini Flower Fritters

Known to the Calabrese as "piteie cu' fiore," these zucchini flower fritters are my favorite summer appetizer. My mother would gather the zucchini flowers from our garden each morning and make these for our family. While it seems this recipe makes a lot of fritters, once your family and friends start eating them, you'll find the plate quickly empties.

Makes about 3 dozen

3 medium Yukon potatoes

2 small zucchini (about 1 pound)

1 teaspoon sea salt

3 garlic cloves, minced, optional

25 to 35 zucchini flowers

1 cup fresh basil, finely chopped

1 cup freshly grated cheese (Parmigiano Reggiano, Grana Padano, or Pecorino Romano), plus more for serving

2 large eggs

1 hot dry sausage, minced, optional

3 cups unbleached all-purpose flour, sifted

4 cups pure olive oil, for frying

Wash, peel, and cut the potatoes into quarters. Wash the zucchini, remove and discard top and bottom stems, and cut into 1-inch slices.

Place 3 cups of water, the potatoes, the zucchini, and salt in a pot and bring to a boil. Continue cooking on medium heat for about 15 minutes or until the vegetables are soft. Remove with a slotted spoon, place in a large bowl, and mash with a fork or potato masher. Reserve 1 cup of the cooking water and set aside. Add the garlic, mix well, and set aside.

For the zucchini flowers, remove and discard the inner pistils and stems. Gently rinse flowers individually in cold water and place in a colander. Set aside.

To the potato-zucchini batter, add basil, cheese, eggs, sausage, flour, and the reserved cooking water. Mix all ingredients well, add the zucchini flowers, and continue mixing. The batter should be the consistency of a thick pancake batter. If needed, add additional flour or water to create this consistency. Let sit for 30 minutes.

In a 13-inch pan, heat oil (about ½-inch in depth) for 3 to 4 minutes on medium heat. To test the oil, place a pinch of the batter in the oil; if it begins to sizzle, the oil is ready. In batches, place heaping tablespoons of batter in the oil, making sure not to overcrowd. When edges begin to turn golden brown, flip and fry the other side. Remove from the pan and place on a paper towel-lined dish to absorb excess oil.

Serve warm or at room temperature with additional freshly grated cheese.

Note: While best served warm, this recipe can be refrigerated overnight and served at room temperature the following day. They can also be frozen for up to 1 week and then thawed at room temperature (rather than reheating).

Serves 6

1 pound frozen porcini mushrooms

2 large eggs

¼ cup freshly grated cheese (Parmi-giano Reggiano, Grana Padano, or Pecorino Romano)

⅛ cup fresh parsley, finely chopped

¼ teaspoon freshly ground black pepper

2 cups breadcrumbs, for coating

3 cups pure olive oil, for frying

Funghi Porcini Fritti

Fried Porcini Mushrooms

When I was young, we imported canned porcini mushrooms preserved in a saltwater brine. Today, porcini mushrooms are available in many specialty stores. The unique flavor of porcini mushrooms makes this appetizer a family favorite.

Let mushrooms thaw for about 2 hours and then rinse in cold water. Pat dry.

Chop each mushroom into 3 slices (smaller mushrooms may be cut into 2).

Beat together eggs, cheese, parsley, and pepper.

Dip mushrooms in egg mixture and then in breadcrumbs. Set aside.

In a 12-inch frying pan, add oil (about ½-inch in depth) and heat for a few minutes on medium-high heat. To test the oil, place a pinch of the mixture in the oil; if it begins to sizzle, the oil is ready. Add mushrooms in a single layer, reduce heat slightly, and fry until golden brown on all sides. Remove from the pan and place on a paper towel-lined dish to absorb excess oil.

Serve warm or at room temperature.

Insalata di Mare
Seafood Salad

Seafood Salad is always served on Christmas Eve. The key to this recipe is individually boiling each fish. The best seafood salad was made by Nino's Restaurant on Coney Island Avenue in Brooklyn, which was owned by a fellow Calabrese. We would always order the seafood salad. This was the one and only catered food my mother would allow in her kitchen.

Serves 4 to 6

1 pound squid tentacles, cleaned

1 pound squid bodies, cleaned and cut in ½-inch rings

1 pound medium shrimp, cleaned and deveined

3¾ teaspoons sea salt, plus more for serving

2 garlic cloves, sliced

¾ cup celery stalks with leaves, finely sliced

½ tablespoon dry Italian oregano

Juice of 1 lemon, freshly squeezed (2 to 3 tablespoons)

⅓ cup extra virgin olive oil, plus more for serving

Place squid tentacles in a pot with 6 cups of cold water and ½ tablespoon salt and bring to a boil. Continue cooking uncovered until tender, about 10 minutes. Drain well, discard water, and set aside.

Place squid rings and ½ tablespoon salt in a pot with 6 cups of cold water and bring to a boil. Continue cooking until tender, about 20 minutes. Drain well, discard water, and set aside.

Place shrimp in a pot with 6 cups of cold water and bring to a boil. Continue cooking for 2 minutes. Drain well, discard water, and set aside.

In a serving bowl, mix tentacles, rings, and shrimp. Add garlic, celery, oregano, ¾ teaspoon salt, and mix well. Add lemon juice and oil, then mix well.

Refrigerate for at least 2 hours before serving. If desired, add additional oil and salt to taste.

Serves 8 to 12

1 honeydew or cantaloupe, chilled

½ pound prosciutto di Parma (about 12 slices)

Prosciutto con Melone

Prosciutto with Melon

Prosciutto with Melon is a great appetizer and simple to prepare.

The contrasting flavors from the fresh, ripe melon and thinly sliced

prosciutto di Parma make this a staple at many parties.

Cut the melon in half, and then remove and discard the seeds. Cut each half into 2-inch-thick slices. For each slice, cut a slit above the rind, cutting all the way through for about ¾ of the slice. There should still be a small piece of melon connected to the rind.

On a platter, place one slice of prosciutto on top of each melon slice. Serve chilled.

Polpo alla Griglia
Grilled Octopus

The secret to this recipe is placing a wine cork in the water and dipping the octopus three times before letting it boil. The natural enzymes from the cork act as a tenderizer, leaving you with a perfectly cooked octopus.

Rinse the octopus in cold water.

Place 5 quarts of cold water in a pot with the cork and bring to a boil. Use a long pair of tongs to hold the octopus and fully dip it into the boiling water 3 times. After the third dip, submerge the octopus and leave to boil for about 45 minutes or until tender. Remove from the pot and set aside.

Preheat the barbecue grill to 500°F. Grill the octopus for about 3 minutes on each side. Let cool for about 15 minutes.

Slice the octopus into 1-inch pieces. In a serving bowl, mix with onion and season with lemon juice, oil, and salt to taste.

Serve warm or at room temperature.

Serves 4

2 fresh or frozen octopus (about 2½ pounds each)

1 natural wine cork

½ small red onion, thinly sliced

Juice of 2 lemons, freshly squeezed (4 to 6 tablespoons)

¼ cup extra virgin olive oil, for seasoning

Sea salt, for seasoning

Serves 10 to 12

1 pound Pecorino Toscano

1 pound Soresina Silano cheese

1 pound soppressata

16 ounces Pickled Eggplant (see page 242)

16 ounces Sun-Dried Tomatoes in Oil (see page 247)

1 pound Fresh Cracked Green Olives (see page 241)

1½ pounds baby artichokes in oil

Antipasto di Formaggio Assortito, Soppressata e Verdure Sott'aceto

Antipasto of Assorted Cheese, Soppressata, and Pickled Vegetables

While charcuterie boards are all the buzz nowadays, I've been making antipasto platters filled with assorted meats, cheeses, and pickled vegetables since I was in elementary school. The rule of thumb is ¼-pound of cheese and salami per person. My favorite cheeses are pecorino toscano, Soresina Silano, Parmigiano-Reggiano (Red Cow), Italian fontina, and Italian Asiago. This recipe is a guideline for antipasto platters. The great thing about this dish is the ability to add your own personal touch to the ingredients you use.

Slice the cheeses and soppressata. Arrange on a serving platter.

Place the vegetables on a separate platter so their oils do not leak onto the meat and cheese.

Soups

Zuppa di Scarola, Cicoria e Finocchio
Escarole, Chicory, and Fennel Soup

Stracciatella
Escarole Egg Drop Soup

Zuppa di Zucchine e Pomodoro
Zucchini and Tomato Soup

Minestra di Cucuzza
Italian Summer Squash Soup

Minestra di Verdura
Mixed Vegetable Soup

Brodo di Manzo
Beef Soup

Brodo di Pollo con Polpettine
Chicken Soup with Little Meatballs

During the winter months, we often had beef or chicken soup for weeknight dinner—but never if we had company. We enjoyed the broth as a first course instead of pasta, followed by the meat or chicken. In making soup, we never used processed bouillon or stock as a base or seasoning. To this day, I use my mother's double-boil method which creates a light and delicate broth. The chicken or beef is placed in a pot with cold water and, as soon as the water begins to boil, the meat is immediately removed and added to a second pot of boiling water and vegetables. When you use this method, you never need to skim the soup to remove impurities or fat during cooking.

Pastina and broken long pasta were the garnishes of choice for broths. They were always boiled separately, drained, and then placed back into the pot. The soup was then ladled into the pastina pot. By cooking it this way, we avoided a starchy broth and any leftover soup could be reheated later with fresh pastina.

Vegetable soups are much lighter, quicker to make, and always flavored with olive oil and grated cheese, sometimes even with eggs. Most vegetable soups were prepared in the summer when we could pick the ingredients from our garden. In a true Calabrese minestra, we use a broken long pasta, such as spaghettini, linguine, or perciatelli, and cook it together with the vegetables. A zuppa does not have pasta.

Zuppa di Scarola, Cicoria e Finocchio

Escarole, Chicory, and Fennel Soup

This soup can be made with escarole alone. However, the combination of the three vegetables creates a uniquely flavored dish. Whenever someone had a stomachache or cold, my mother would always prepare this soup. She knew that the broth created from these vegetables was better than any medicine.

Serves 6

2 heads escarole (about 2 pounds)

2 bunches chicory (about 2 pounds)

1 fennel bulb with leaves and stems (about 1 pound)

2 teaspoons sea salt

Freshly grated cheese (Parmigiano-Reggiano, Grana Padano, or Pecorino Romano), for serving

Extra virgin olive oil, for serving

Discard the escarole stem. Wash the individual leaves in cold water, and then cut into 2-inch pieces. Rewash the cut escarole 3 to 4 times in cold water. Repeat this step for the chicory.

For the fennel, separate the stems and leaves from the bulb. Cut the leaves and stems into 1-inch pieces and rinse well. (The bulb is not used in this recipe but can be eaten on its own or used in salads.)

Place 2½ quarts of cold water in a large pot and bring to a boil. Then add escarole, chicory, fennel stems and leaves, and salt. Continue cooking for about 1 hour.

Serve immediately with a spoonful of freshly grated cheese and drizzle of oil to each individual serving.

Stracciatella
Escarole Egg Drop Soup

This is the Calabrese version of Roman Egg Drop Soup. The escarole can be boiled in the morning and the egg mixture can be added about 30 minutes before serving.

Serves 4 to 6

2 large heads escarole (about 3 pounds)

1½ teaspoons sea salt

2 large eggs

1 cup freshly grated cheese (Parmigiano Reggiano, Grana Padano, or Pecorino Romano), plus more for serving

4 tablespoons extra virgin olive oil, plus more for serving

Discard the escarole stems. Wash the individual leaves in cold water, then cut into 1-inch pieces. Rewash the cut escarole 3 to 4 times in cold water.

Bring 10 cups of cold water to a boil, add escarole and salt, and bring back to a boil. Reduce heat to a medium-low simmer, and continue cooking semi-covered for about 1 hour. Occasionally use a spoon to push down the escarole beneath the water's surface.

Once the escarole is cooked, beat the eggs, cheese, and oil in a separate bowl until the eggs are pale yellow in color and slightly frothy.

Increase the simmering pot to high heat, add the egg mixture, and stir vigorously for 1 to 2 minutes. Continue cooking for 5 to 7 minutes, until the egg is fully cooked.

Serve immediately with additional freshly grated cheese and oil to taste.

Zuppa di Zucchine e Pomodoro
Zucchini and Tomato Soup

This simple soup is best in summer months. For those who have been convinced that chicken or vegetable stocks are the only way to go when making soup, this zuppa will be an eye-opening experience. By using the precise amount of water, a more flavorful broth is created allowing seasonal ingredients and flavors to showcase in a way that other broths would hide.

Serves 6

3 plum tomatoes, seeded, cored, and cut into quarters

14 fresh basil leaves, chopped

12 small zucchini, cut in half and then into 1-inch pieces (about 3½ pounds)

2 teaspoons sea salt

¼ cup freshly grated cheese (Parmigiano Reggiano, Grana Padano, or Pecorino Romano), plus more for serving

2 tablespoons extra virgin olive oil, plus more for serving

Place tomatoes, basil, and salt in a pot with 7½ cups of cold water. Bring to a boil.

Add zucchini. Continue to cook semi-covered until the vegetables are tender, about 25 minutes.

Add cheese and oil. Mix well and continue cooking for another 2 to 3 minutes.

Serve immediately with additional freshly grated cheese and oil to taste.

Serves 6

2 cucuzza (Italian summer squash) (about 4 pounds)

6 leaves fresh basil, chopped

1½ teaspoons sea salt

¼ pound spaghettini pasta, broken into small pieces

1 large egg

¾ cup freshly grated cheese (Parmigiana Reggiano, Grana Padano, or Pecorino Romano), plus more for serving

1 tablespoon extra virgin olive oil

Minestra di Cucuzza

Italian Summer Squash Soup

The squash used in this recipe is called cucuzza. We always grew it in our backyard during the summer months. This squash was pale green in color and some grew several feet long. Unlike zucchini, the skin was very tough and needed to be peeled and discarded before cooking. The leaves of this plant were chopped and added to different minestre during the summer. This plant also produces flowers, which are used for the Zucchini Flower Fritters (see page 40). My mother would never pick the first cucuzza of the season. Instead, she would let it grow until the end of the season and remove its seeds to use the following year for planting. This recipe was usually made with capellini pasta, but I prefer to prepare it with spaghettini, which is a little thicker.

For the cucuzza, slice off and discard the top and bottom. Then peel off the skin. With a knife, cut in half vertically. Scoop out and discard the seeds and some pulp. Cut the remaining cucuzza into cubes, rinse, and set aside.

Place the basil in a pot with 8 cups of cold water, bring to a boil, and then add cucuzza and salt. Continue to cook on high heat until it returns to a boil.

Reduce heat to medium and continue cooking semi-covered for 10 minutes or until the cucuzza is tender. Add pasta and continue cooking on medium heat, stirring occasionally to make sure the pasta does not clump. Cook until the pasta is al dente.

In a separate bowl, beat the egg, cheese, and oil until slightly frothy.

Increase the pot's heat to high and add the egg mixture, stirring continuously and cook for about 5 minutes.

Let sit for a few minutes before serving with additional freshly grated cheese and oil to taste.

Serves 6

2 plum tomatoes, seeded, cored, and cut into quarters

6 leaves fresh basil, chopped

2 teaspoons sea salt

1 large Yukon potato, peeled and cut into cubes

2 medium zucchini, cut into cubes (about 1 pound)

½ pound string beans, top and tail removed and cut into halves

10 leaves escarole, chopped into 1-inch pieces

¼ fennel bulb with leaves and stems, chopped

½ pound spaghettini or linguine fine

2 tablespoons extra virgin olive oil

2 tablespoons freshly grated cheese (Parmigiano Reggiano, Grana Padano, or Pecorino Romano), plus more for serving

Minestra di Verdura

Mixed Vegetable Soup

The secret to this recipe is the precise amount of water. If there is too much water, the soup is not flavorful. If there is not enough water, the soup is too starchy. Although minestra always contains tomato and basil, any additional combination of fresh vegetables can be used.

In a pot with 3 quarts of cold water, place tomatoes, basil, and salt and bring to a boil.

Add the potato, zucchini, string beans, escarole, and fennel and bring to a boil. Continue cooking on medium-low heat for about 25 minutes.

Break the pasta into 3-inch pieces, add it to the pot, mix well, and continue cooking about 10 minutes or until the pasta is cooked.

Add oil and cheese and mix well.

Serve immediately with additional freshly grated cheese and oil to taste.

Serves 6 to 8

3 pieces of beef shank with bone (about 4 pounds total)

2 large carrots, peeled and chopped into large slices

2 large onions, sliced

3 celery stalks, chopped

¼ cup fresh parsley, chopped

1 garlic clove

3½ teaspoons sea salt

1 pound perciatelli or bucatini pasta

Freshly grated cheese (Parmigiano Reggiano, Grana Padano or Pecorino Romano), for serving

Brodo di Manzo
Beef Soup

This was my father's favorite soup and we always made it during the winter months. Although it can be made with any small pasta shape, his favorite was broken bucatini or perciatelli. The meat in the soup can be eaten as a side dish or placed back in the broth for extra beef flavor.

In a large pot with 8 cups of cold water, place beef shanks and cook on medium heat until the water begins to boil. Remove the beef shanks, place in a colander, and set aside.

In a separate large pot with 6 quarts of cold water, place carrots, onion, celery, parsley, garlic, and salt and bring to a boil.

Add the beef shanks and continue to cook until the water returns to a boil. Reduce to a low simmer and cook semi-covered for about 2 hours and 15 minutes or until the meat falls off the bone and is tender. Remove from heat and let sit covered for 30 minutes.

In a separate pot large enough for the full soup, bring 3 quarts of water to a boil. Break the pasta into 2-inch pieces and cook according to directions on package. Drain well and let sit in colander.

Remove about half of the meat from the soup, cut into small pieces, and place back into the soup.

Add two ladles of soup to the empty pasta pot, cook on high heat for 2 minutes, and then add the pasta. Add any additional soup until the pasta is covered. Continue to cook for 3 to 4 minutes. (Any remaining beef shank can be served as a side dish to the soup.)

Serve immediately with freshly grated cheese.

Serves 6 to 8

1 whole chicken (about 3.5 pounds), cut into eighths

4½ dozen mini Meatballs, uncooked (see page 173)

3 large carrots, peeled and thickly sliced

3 celery stalks with leaves, sliced

1 large onion, sliced

2 tablespoons fresh parsley, finely chopped

1 garlic clove

3 teaspoons sea salt

1 pound pastina or soup pasta

Freshly grated cheese (Parmigiano Reggiano, Grana Padano, or Pecorino Romano), for serving

Brodo di Pollo con Polpettine

Chicken Soup with Little Meatballs

There is nothing like a dish of homemade chicken soup on a cold winter night. As a young girl, my mother used to bring me to Lapera Bros. Poultry on 61st Street in Brooklyn. She would pick out her chickens, looking for the plumpest ones. At home, she would wash and soak them in a saltwater brine and then freeze them. My mother would always tell me, "Fresh chickens are best if frozen before cooking."

Prepare Meatballs according to recipe, reducing the recipe in half and setting aside the uncooked mini meatballs once formed.

Wash chicken and remove and discard about half of the skin and fat. In a large pot with 8 cups of cold water, place chicken and begin cooking on medium-high heat. When the water begins to boil, immediately transfer the chicken to a colander and discard the water.

Place 5 quarts of cold water in a large pot, add carrots, celery, onion, parsley, garlic, and salt and bring to a boil. Add uncooked meatballs and bring to a boil. Then, add chicken and continue to cook on medium-low heat, semi-covered for about 2 hours. Turn off heat and let sit for about 30 minutes.

Remove chicken from the pot. Remove and discard the bones from the chicken. With a fork, shred the chicken and place back in the pot. Continue cooking for another 3 to 4 minutes. (Alternatively, only shred half the chicken and serve the other half on its own as a side to the soup.)

In a separate large pot, bring water to a boil. Add pastina and cook according to directions on package. Drain well and let sit in colander.

Return the soup to a boil. Add about 3 ladles of soup to the empty pastina pot and heat for about 1 minute on high heat. Then add the cooked pastina. Mix well and add additional soup as desired.

Serve immediately with freshly grated cheese.

Legumes

Lenticchie
Lentils

Fave Secche con la Buccia
Dried Fava with Skin

Ceci
Chickpeas

Fagioli Cannellini
Cannellini Beans

Legumes, such as cannellini, borlotti, fava, chickpeas, and lentils, are usually eaten in the winter months as a first course topped with olive oil or mixed with small pasta shapes like tubettini or mini shells. They are also sometimes served as a side dish to the meat course.

In Calabria, legumes were always cooked over low heat in clay pots. The taste of freshly made legumes is incomparably better than that of canned or jarred ones. We only add olive oil to those we plan to eat immediately. Once you begin cooking dried legumes, you will realize how easy it is. You can store them in the refrigerator for up to two days or freeze them for a few weeks, as long as you haven't added oil. Leftovers are a great addition to soups or can be stirred into pasta.

Lenticchie
Lentils

In Italy, we cook lentils on New Year's Eve and eat them after midnight in order to bring good luck and prosperity. My two favorite lentils are lentils from Castelluccio and Umbria.

Serves 4 to 6

1 pound Italian dry lentils (Umbria or Castelluccio)

1 large carrot, peeled and sliced

1 celery stalk, sliced

1 medium onion, sliced

1½ teaspoons sea salt

Extra virgin olive oil, for seasoning

Vinegar peppers, sliced, optional for serving

Hot peppers in oil, sliced, optional for serving

Rinse lentils in cold water and drain in colander.

Place 7 cups of cold water in a pot with carrot, celery, onion, and salt and bring to a boil.

Add lentils to the pot and return to a boil. Continue cooking on medium-low heat semi-covered for 40 to 50 minutes or until tender. Stir occasionally to make sure the lentils do not stick to the bottom of the pot.

Remove from heat and let sit covered for 10 minutes.

Serve with oil to taste and, if desired, vinegar or hot peppers.

Note: Cooking time may vary for all beans. If additional cooking time is needed, add 1 to 2 ladles of boiling water, stir, and continue cooking.

Serves 4 to 6

1 pound dry fava beans (with skin)
1 medium onion, sliced
1½ teaspoons sea salt
Extra virgin olive oil, for serving

Fave Secche con la Buccia

Dried Fava with Skin

All legumes can be served as a primo piatto, instead of pasta or soup. I prefer this legume as a side dish for grilled meats. The fava beans must be soaked overnight before cooking. Many recipes call for removing the skins of the fava beans, but the Calabrese always eat them with the skin on, regardless of whether or not the beans are fresh or dried.

Rinse fava beans in cold water. Place in a large bowl with cold water, at least 4 inches above the beans as they will absorb most of the water during the night. Soak overnight. The next day, drain beans and discard the water.

Using a knife, cut a 1/8-inch slit on the side of each fava.

In a large pot with 8 cups of cold water, add onion and salt and bring to a boil. Add beans and cook, semi-covered on medium-low heat for about 1 hour and 20 minutes. Stir occasionally to make sure the beans do not stick to the bottom of the pot.

Let sit for 10 minutes. Serve with oil to taste.

Note: Cooking time may vary for all beans. If additional cooking time is needed, add 1 to 2 ladles of boiling water, stir, and continue cooking.

Serves 4 to 6

1 pound Italian dry chickpeas
1 medium onion, chopped
1 large carrot, peeled and sliced
1 garlic clove
⅛ teaspoon baking soda
2 teaspoons sea salt
Extra virgin olive oil, for serving

Ceci

Chickpeas

Chickpeas are one of the most popular legumes produced world-wide. By soaking them overnight, you can soften the chickpeas and make them more digestible. Another trick is to add a very small amount of baking soda, which will shorten the cooking time.

Rinse chickpeas in cold water. Place in a bowl with about 6 cups of cold water and soak overnight. The next day, drain chickpeas and discard the water.

Place 6 cups of cold water in a pot. Add onion, carrot, garlic, and baking soda and bring to a boil. Add chickpeas and salt and bring to a boil.

Continue cooking on medium-low heat semi-covered for about 1 hour or until the chickpeas are tender. Stir occasionally to make sure they do not stick to the bottom of the pot.

Serve warm and top with oil to taste.

Note: Cooking time may vary for all beans. If additional cooking time is needed, add 1 to 2 ladles of boiling water, stir, and continue cooking.

1 pound Italian dry cannellini beans

1 large carrot, peeled and sliced

1 medium onion, sliced

1 celery stalk, chopped

1 garlic clove

2 teaspoons sea salt

Extra virgin olive oil, for seasoning

Vinegar peppers, sliced, optional for serving

Hot peppers in oil, sliced, optional for serving

Fagioli Cannellini

Cannellini Beans

Cannellini beans are my favorite legume. Even though overnight soaking is required, this recipe is very easy to make. It also works well with dried borlotti beans.

Rinse beans in cold water. Place in a large bowl with cold water, at least 2 inches above the beans. Soak overnight. The next day, drain beans and discard the water.

Place 2½ quarts of cold water, carrot, onion, celery, and garlic in a pot and bring to a boil. Add beans and salt and return to a boil. Reduce to low heat and continue to cook, semi-covered, for about 1 hour and 15 minutes. Stir occasionally to make sure the beans do not stick to the bottom of the pot.

Remove from heat and let sit for 10 minutes. Serve with oil to taste and, if desired, vinegar or hot peppers.

Note: Cooking time may vary for all beans. If additional cooking time is needed, add 1 to 2 ladles of boiling water, stir, and continue cooking.

Pasta:

Pasta Plus a Second Course

Sugo di Domenica con Polpette e Salsiccia
Sunday Sauce with Meatballs and Sausage

Sugo di Maiale con Polpette e Salsiccia
Pork Sauce with Meatballs and Sausage

Sugo di Agnello
Lamb Sauce

Sugo di Carciofi Ripiene
Stuffed Artichoke Sauce

Sugo di Stoccafisso
Stockfish Sauce

Sugo all'Aragosta Fra Diavolo
Lobster Sauce Fra Diavolo

What would an Italian cookbook be without a pasta section? Legend has it that back in the day, a Calabrese woman needed to know how to make fifteen different pasta dishes. If you were raised by someone like my mother, that wasn't a difficult thing to accomplish.

Pasta is my favorite food and it's extremely versatile. It can be served as the primo or secondo piatto. You can make a simple spaghetti with tomato, onion, and olive oil in just fifteen minutes, or spend several hours preparing a baked ziti.

In the Calabrese kitchen, there are lots of rules about pasta. There is no such thing as egg pasta. Long pasta is never broken into pieces if it's served with sauce but can be broken if it's being added to soups or minestra. Like all Italian cooks, we're fanatical about which pasta cut we pair with which sauce. When you walk through Coluccio's, you can tell which region of Italy customers are from by the cuts of pasta in their shopping baskets.

When I make pasta, it usually involves tomatoes. Give me a can of tomatoes and I can make you anything! I use three different types: whole peeled Italian tomatoes, passata di pomodoro (tomato purée), or canned Italian cherry tomatoes. You can't substitute one for another. Each has its own relative thickness and therefore its own cooking time.

I always cook pasta in an abundant amount of water, stirring it in after the water comes to a rolling boil, and then adding a generous amount of salt. Pasta is always cooked al dente, or to the tooth.

After the pasta is cooked, I immediately drain the pasta in a colander, place it back in the pot, and then ladle in sauce until all of the pasta has absorbed the sauce. To avoid the pasta from drowning in sauce, I never add the pasta directly to the sauce. This first pasta chapter includes sauces that are primarily flavored with meats, fish, or vegetables. These sauces provide a dual purpose: the meat, fish, or vegetable are removed from the pot and served as a secondo piatto and the sauce is served to accompany the pasta. Meat sauces are always served with thicker pasta cuts like penne, rigatoni, ziti, or Filei Calabrese. Fish sauces are tossed with long pasta, such as spaghetti or linguine. The thinner cuts of these pastas—spaghettini and linguine fine—are only served when cooking less than one pound of pasta, as it is too difficult to make sure large amounts are al dente. Onion, garlic, hot red pepper, and basil create the base for most meat and vegetable sauces while garlic, hot red pepper, and parsley are the starting ingredients for fish sauces. I always begin sautéing in a cold pot, using whole cloves of garlic and thickly sliced onions to prevent them from burning. When the sauce is done, I discard the garlic. My Zio Rocco, my mother's brother, who was an incredible cook, always said "The garlic should be tasted and not seen." The hot pepper adds a distinct flavor and doesn't make the sauce spicy, unless you break it up during the cooking process.

Serves 5 to 6

5 links fresh Italian sausage (hot or sweet)

1/3 cup extra virgin olive oil

1 medium onion, sliced

1 garlic clove

5 fresh basil leaves, chopped

1 small hot red pepper, optional

½ teaspoon sea salt

2 28-ounce cans Italian whole peeled tomatoes

13 medium Meatballs, uncooked (see page 173)

1½ pounds pasta (Filei Calabrese, penne rigate, or spaghetti)

Freshly grated cheese (Parmigiano Reggiano, Grana Padano, or Pecorino Romano), for serving

Sugo di Domenica con Polpette e Salsiccia

Sunday Sauce with Meatballs and Sausage

I make this dish every Sunday for my family. The sauce is made early in the morning, and I cook the pasta later in the day. The uncooked meatballs are added directly into the simmering sauce. At the end of the evening, we refrigerate any leftover meatballs and sauce for dinner the following night.

Place sausage in a pot, cover with cold water, and begin cooking on medium-high heat. When the water begins to boil, remove the sausage and place in a colander. Pierce the sausage a few times with a fork. Discard the water.

In a 6-quart pot, sauté oil, onion, garlic, basil, and hot pepper (if using) for 2 minutes on medium heat. Add sausage and salt then continue to sauté for another 3 or 4 minutes, continuously stirring.

Using a vegetable mill, purée the tomatoes and then add to pot. Rinse the can with ¼ cup of water and add to pot. Raise the heat to medium-high and continue to cook until the sauce begins to boil.

Add uncooked meatballs to the simmering sauce, stir, and continue to cook uncovered on medium heat until the sauce returns to a boil. Reduce heat and continue to cook on a low simmer, semi-covered for about 1 hour and 30 minutes, stirring occasionally. Let sit for about 15 minutes.

When preparing to serve, reheat the sauce, and remove the meatballs and sausage (to be served as a secondo piatto to the pasta).

In a separate pot, bring water to a boil. Add pasta and cook for according to directions on package. Drain well.

Return the drained pasta to the empty pot and ladle sauce into the pot. Mix well on medium-high until the sauce fully coats the pasta.

Serve immediately with freshly grated cheese.

Note: You can make a fresh, quick meat sauce with any leftover sauce. Heat the sauce with sausage or meatballs, add 1 26-ounce bottle of passata di pomodoro and 1 tablespoon oil, and then cook on low heat for about 15 minutes. This sauce is enough for 1 pound of pasta and serves 4. Leftover sauce is good for up to 2 days refrigerated.

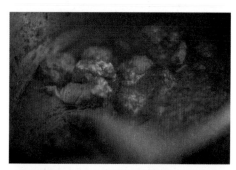

Serves 8 to 12

2 2½ pounds country-style spare ribs

8 to 10 links fresh Italian sausage (hot or sweet)

¾ cup extra virgin olive oil

2 medium onions, sliced

2 garlic cloves

12 fresh basil leaves, chopped

1 small hot red pepper, optional

teaspoon freshly ground black pepper

½ teaspoon sea salt

5 28-ounce cans Italian whole peeled tomatoes

13 medium Meatballs, uncooked (see page 173)

2 pounds pasta (penne rigate, rigatoni, or spaghetti)

Freshly grated Cheese (Parmigiano Reggiano, Grana Padano, or Pecorino Romano), for serving

Sugo di Maiale con Polpette e Salsiccia

Pork Sauce with Meatballs and Sausage

This is a typical ragu, which my mother made on Sundays. Every Sunday she would wake up early to go to mass, then come home and prepare the sauce for an early afternoon dinner. My fondest memories of Sunday afternoons were going to the pot when the sauce was ready. I would take a bowl and add some sauce, a meatball, spare rib, and sausage. Then I would get a large piece of bread and begin eating. "Why can't you wait to eat this with the pasta in a few hours?" my mother would always ask. I would reply, "It doesn't taste the same when it isn't eaten right away!"

Place sausage and pork ribs in a pot, cover with cold water, and begin cooking on medium-high heat. When water begins to boil, remove sausage and pork immediately and place in a colander. Pierce the sausage a few times with a fork. Discard the water.

In a large pot, sauté oil, onion, garlic, basil, and hot pepper (if using) for 2 minutes on medium heat. Add pork meat, sausage, black pepper, and salt and continue to sauté another 3 to 4 minutes, continuously stirring.

Using a vegetable mill, purée the tomatoes and then add to pot. Rinse the can with ¼ cup of water and add to pot. Raise the heat to medium-high and continue to cook until the sauce begins to boil.

Add uncooked meatballs to the simmering sauce, stir, and continue to cook uncovered on medium heat until the sauce returns to a boil again. Reduce heat and continue to cook on a lower simmer, semi-covered for about 2 hours, stirring occasionally. The sauce is ready when the pork meat easily falls from the bone and oil rises to the top of the pot. Let sit for about 15 minutes.

When preparing to serve, reheat the sauce and remove sausage, pork, and meatballs (to be served as a secondo piatto to the pasta).

In a separate pot, bring water to a boil. Add pasta and cook according to directions on package. Drain well.

Place the drained pasta back into the empty pot and ladle sauce in the pot. Mix well on medium-high until the sauce fully coats the pasta.

Serve immediately with freshly grated cheese.

Note: Country-style pork ribs are recommended for the pork meat. If they are not available, baby back ribs or pork chops with a bone (cut in half) can be used.

Note: To make a fresh, quick meat sauce with any leftover sauce, heat the sauce with sausage or meatballs, add 1 26-ounce bottle of passata di pomodoro and 1 tablespoon oil, then cook on low heat for about 15 minutes. This sauce is enough for 1 pound of pasta and serves 4. Leftover sauce is good for up to 2 days refrigerated.

Variation: Pork skin can be added to the pork sauce with pork meat. In Calabria, this is known as "adding fringá" to the sauce. Take a piece of pork skin about 8 inches in length and place in a pot with 4 cups of cold water and 2 teaspoons salt. Bring to a boil and let cook for approximately 30 minutes. Remove the pork skin and discard water. Add the pork skin to the sauce about 30 minutes before the sauce is ready. When the sauce is ready, remove the skin, slice into 2-inch pieces, and serve as a secondo piatto with the pork meat, sausage, and meatballs.

Serves 8

3 pounds baby lamb pieces, assorted

1 cup red wine

1 large onion, sliced

½ cup fresh parsley, chopped

3 fresh basil leaves, chopped

4 garlic cloves

½ cup extra virgin olive oil

1 small hot red pepper, optional

1 teaspoon sea salt

1/8 teaspoon freshly ground black pepper

3 28-ounce cans Italian whole peeled tomatoes

2 pounds pasta (ziti, pennoni lisce, mostaccioli, or long ziti)

Freshly grated cheese (Parmigiano Reggiano, Grana Padano, or Pecorino Romano), for serving

Sugo di Agnello

Lamb Sauce

We always made lamb sauce on either Palm Sunday or Easter Sunday. Typically, this dish was made with lamb and potatoes baked in the oven. The lamb in this recipe can be substituted with goat. The pasta used is typically a short cut without lines, also known as pasta lisce.

Wash the lamb pieces in cold water, rinsing several times.

In a large pot with 2 cups of cold water, combine wine and the lamb pieces. Begin cooking on medium-high heat. When the water begins to boil, remove the lamb pieces and place in a colander and set aside. Discard the water.

In an 11-quart pot, sauté onion, parsley, basil, garlic, oil, and hot pepper (if using) for about 3 minutes on medium heat.

Add the lamb pieces, salt, and black pepper, mix all the ingredients Continue to cook on medium heat semi-covered for about 12 minutes, stirring occasionally.

Using a vegetable mill, purée the tomatoes. Add puréed tomatoes to pot and raise the heat to medium high. Continue to cook until the sauce begins to boil.

Reduce heat to medium-low and continue to cook, semi-covered for about 2 hours, stirring occasionally. Sauce is cooked when the lamb meat easily falls off the bone. Let sit for about 30 minutes.

When preparing to serve, reheat sauce, and remove lamb pieces (to be used as a secondo piatto to the pasta).

In a separate pot, bring water to a boil. Add pasta and cook according to directions on package. Drain well.

Return the drained pasta to the empty pot and ladle sauce into the pot. Mix well on medium-high heat until the sauce fully coats the pasta.

Serve immediately with freshly grated cheese.

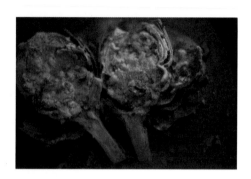

Serves 4 to 6

Stuffed artichokes:

½ cup breadcrumbs

¼ cup freshly grated cheese (Parmigiano Reggiano, Grana Padano, or Pecorino Romano)

¼ cup fresh parsley, finely chopped

1 garlic clove, minced

1 tablespoon extra virgin olive oil

2 ounces mozzarella cheese, shredded

6 medium or 8 baby artichokes

1 lemon, cut into quarters

1 teaspoon sea salt

Sewing thread, optional

Sauce:

½ cup extra virgin olive oil

1 medium onion, sliced

1 garlic clove

3 fresh basil leaves, chopped

2 28-ounce cans Italian whole peeled tomatoes

½ teaspoon sea salt

1 pound pasta (penne rigate, ziti, spaghetti, or tagliatelle)

Freshly grated cheese (Parmigiano Reggiano, Grana Padano, Pecorino Romano), for serving

Sugo di Carciofi Ripiene

Stuffed Artichoke Sauce

This sauce was usually made in the spring on Wednesday or Friday nights. This recipe works well with medium or baby artichokes. The stuffed artichokes in the sauce are great as a side dish to pasta or as a secondo piatto.

For the stuffed artichokes:

In a bowl, mix breadcrumbs, grated cheese, parsley, garlic, oil, and mozzarella. Set aside.

Wash the artichokes and remove and discard about ¼-inch of each stem. Peel the outside of the remaining stem and remove and discard the outer leaves and about 1-inch of the top portion of the artichokes.

In a large pot with 3 quarts of cold water, add artichokes, lemon, and salt and bring to a boil. Continue boiling for 4 to 5 minutes and then immediately remove the artichokes and place on a dish.

Gently open the leaves of the artichokes and use your hands to stuff each leaf with the stuffing mix.

If using the sewing thread, wrap the thread around each artichoke and tightly knot to prevent the stuffing from falling out. Set aside.

For the sauce:

In a large pot, sauté oil, onion, garlic, and basil for about 2 minutes on medium heat.

Using a vegetable mill, purée the tomatoes. Add puréed tomatoes and salt to the pot and continue to stir.

When the sauce begins to boil, add the artichokes and continue cooking on medium-low heat for about 35 minutes. Let sit for about 15 minutes.

When preparing to serve, reheat the sauce. Then remove the artichokes and remove and discard the thread wrapped around the artichoke. Set aside and serve as a side dish to the pasta.

In a separate pot, bring water to a boil. Add pasta and cook according to directions on package. Drain well.

Return the drained pasta to the empty pot and ladle sauce into the pot. Mix well on medium-high heat until the sauce fully coats the pasta.

Serve immediately with freshly grated cheese.

Serves 6

1½ pounds dry stockfish

5 tablespoons baking soda

2 medium onions, sliced

4 garlic cloves

2 small red hot or sweet peppers or 2 tablespoons hot pepper paste

½ cup fresh parsley, chopped

½ cup extra virgin olive oil

2 teaspoons sea salt

2 28-ounce cans Italian whole peeled tomatoes

1½ pounds pasta (spaccatelle, bucatini, perciatelli, or linguine)

Sugo di Stoccafisso

Stockfish Sauce

While I was never really a fan of stockfish, the sauce that it creates is incredible. The fish is very high in protein and low in fat. Known as stocco, stockfish is most famously from Mammola in Reggio Calabria. Some say the water in Mammola is the reason this dish is so spectacular. This recipe is usually made with bucatini or perciatelli pasta, but in Sicily they often make it with a shape of pasta called spaccatelle. This sauce should be made in the fall or winter months. You must soak the stockfish for approximately eleven days before it is ready for the sauce.

Soaking the stockfish:

Cut the dry fish in half horizontally and place in a plastic tub filled with cold water. Add 1 tablespoon baking soda. Place in the refrigerator or in a cool place.

Replace the water with fresh cold water each morning and evening. Add fresh baking soda only in the mornings. Continue this process for 5 days.

On the sixth day, cut the fish in half again and continue changing the water in the morning and evening for an additional 5 days. Do not add any additional baking soda at this point.

Remove fish from the water and pat dry. It can be cooked immediately or stored in the refrigerator for up to 3 days. The fish can also be frozen for up to 2 months.

For the stockfish sauce:

Once the stockfish has been soaked, remove fish from refrigerator (or defrost) and pat fish dry with a paper towel.

In a large nonstick sauté pot with lid, sauté onion, garlic, peppers, parsley, and oil for about 4 minutes.

Add fish (skin-side down) and salt to the pot. Continue cooking completely covered on medium-low for 10 minutes. Shake the pan occasionally to make sure the fish does not stick to the bottom of the pan.

Using a vegetable mill, purée the tomatoes. Add puréed tomatoes to the

pot and continue cooking semi-covered on medium-low for about 1 hour. Let sit for about 15 minutes.

When preparing to serve, reheat the sauce and remove the stockfish (to be served as a secondo piatto to the pasta).

In a separate pot, bring water to a boil. Add pasta and cook for according to directions on package. Drain well.

Return the drained pasta to the empty pot and ladle sauce into the pot. Mix well on medium-high heat until the sauce fully coats the pasta.

Serve immediately.

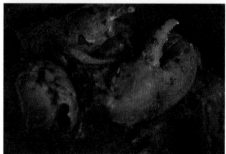

Sugo all'Aragosta Fra Diavolo

Lobster Sauce Fra Diavolo

We always make this sauce on Christmas Eve and New Year's Eve. I love using any remaining sauce to create a new meal on the day after Christmas. I take the remaining lobster sauce and add any leftover Hot Sauce for Fish (see page 107) from the Feast of the Seven Fishes. I then add a container of heavy cream and cook it for five minutes. This new sauce goes great with capellini. While this is not a typical Calabrese dish, my mother always taught me how to turn leftovers into a brand-new meal.

Serves 4

½ cup extra virgin olive oil

4 garlic cloves

2 small hot red peppers or 2 tablespoons hot pepper paste

3 1¼-pound lobsters, cleaned and separated (claws, body, and tail)

½ cup fresh parsley, chopped

2 28-ounce cans Italian whole peeled tomatoes

½ teaspoon sea salt

1 pound pasta (linguine, spaghetti, or fettuccine)

In a 6-quart sauté pot, sauté oil, garlic, and hot pepper for about 1 minute. Remove the garlic and pepper and add the lobsters to the pot. Immediately add the parsley and the removed garlic and pepper back to the pot. (By doing so, you ensure the garlic and peppers do not burn at the bottom of the pot.)

Cook completely covered on low heat for about 20 minutes, shaking the pot occasionally to make sure the lobster does not stick to the bottom of the pot.

Using a vegetable mill, purée the tomatoes. Add puréed tomatoes to pot and continue to cook semi-covered on medium heat. Once the sauce begins to boil, reduce heat and continue cooking for about 40 minutes. Turn off heat and let sit for about 30 minutes.

When preparing to serve, reheat the sauce, crush the hot pepper with a fork, and remove the lobsters (to be served as a secondo piatto to the pasta). Remove and discard the garlic.

In a separate pot, bring water to a boil. Add pasta and cook according to directions on package. Drain well.

Return the drained pasta to the empty pot and ladle sauce into the pot. Mix well on medium-high until the sauce fully coats the pasta.

Serve immediately.

More Pasta:

Quick Dishes and Sauces

Sugo di Pomodoro Schiacciato a Mano
Hand-Crushed Tomato Sauce

Sugo di Pomodoro con Soppressata
Tomato Sauce with Soppressata

Sugo di Gamberi
Shrimp Sauce

Sugo di Vongole con Pomodorini
Clam Sauce with Cherry Tomatoes

Sugo di Funghi Porcini
Porcini Mushroom Sauce

Salsa Piccante per Pesce
Hot Sauce for Fish

Sugo Finto
"Fake Sauce"

Pasta con Broccoli
Pasta with Broccoli

Pasta con Fave e Piselli
Pasta with Fava and Peas

Pasta e Ceci
Pasta and Chickpeas

Pasta con Fagiolini e Patate
Pasta with String Beans and Potatoes

Pasta con Ricotta
Pasta with Ricotta

Pastina con Uovo, Burro e Formaggio
Pastina with Egg, Butter, and Cheese

This is my favorite section of the book because the recipes are easy to make. When families were very large in southern Italy, these dishes were served as the main course, as they were inexpensive and could be prepared with items that were always stocked in the pantry or growing in the garden.

Sugo di Pomodoro Schiacciato a Mano

Hand-Crushed Tomato Sauce

This is a simple and delicious tomato sauce. My mother tended to serve it at family meals because she considered it too rustic to serve to guests. When she prepared the sauce for company, she instead insisted on pressing the tomatoes through a colander or food mill, so the sauce had a smooth and even consistency.

Serves 4

1 medium onion, sliced

1 garlic clove

6 fresh basil leaves, chopped

1 small hot red pepper, optional

⅓ cup extra virgin olive oil

1 28-ounce can Italian whole peeled tomatoes

1 pound pasta (spaghetti, linguine, or penne)

Freshly grated cheese (Parmigiano Reggiano, Grana Padano, or Pecorino Romano), for serving

In a medium sauté pan, sauté the onion, garlic, basil, hot pepper (if using), and oil on medium heat for 3 to 4 minutes.

Add the tomatoes with their juices to the pan and begin smashing the tomatoes with a fork until all the tomatoes are crushed.

Continue cooking on medium-low for about 10 minutes, stirring occasionally.

In a separate pot, bring water to a boil. Add pasta and cook according to directions on package. Drain well.

Return the drained pasta to the empty pot and ladle sauce into the pot. Mix well on medium-high until the sauce fully coats the pasta.

Serve immediately with freshly grated cheese.

Serves 4

1 medium onion, sliced

5 fresh basil leaves, torn in half

⅓ cup extra virgin olive oil

8 thick slices hot soppressata

1 28-ounce can Italian whole peeled tomatoes

1 pound pasta (spaghetti, penne, or tagliatelle)

Freshly grated cheese (Parmigiano Reggiano, Grana Padano, or Pecorino Romano), for serving

Sugo di Pomodoro con Soppressata

Tomato Sauce with Soppressata

While northern Italians prepare this sauce with pancetta or prosciutto, the Calabrese use soppressata. This was my mother's signature sauce that she served when unexpected guests arrived for dinner.

In a medium sauté pan, sauté onion, basil, oil, and soppressata on medium-heat for about 2 minutes.

Using a vegetable mill, purée the tomatoes. Add the puréed tomato to the pan and continue cooking on medium heat until the sauce begins to boil. Stir occasionally.

Reduce heat slightly and continue cooking on a low simmer for another 10 minutes.

In a separate pot, bring water to a boil. Add pasta and cook according to directions on package. Drain well.

Return the drained pasta to the empty pot and ladle sauce into the pot. Mix well on medium-high heat until the sauce fully coats the pasta.

Serve immediately with freshly grated cheese.

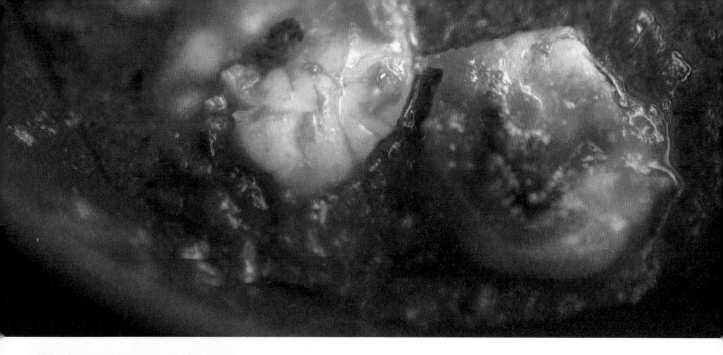

Serves 4

½ cup extra virgin olive oil

½ cup fresh parsley, chopped

4 garlic cloves

1 small hot red pepper, optional

1 pound medium or large shrimp, shelled, cleaned, and deveined

½ teaspoon sea salt

1 28-ounce can Italian whole peeled tomatoes

1 pound pasta (tripoline, linguine, spaghetti, or fettuccine)

Sugo di Gamberi

Shrimp Sauce

My favorite pasta for this sauce is tripolini, a long pasta with ruffles on one side. If you decide to use a red hot pepper in this dish, you can easily create a fra diavolo by crushing the pepper at the end of the cooking.

In a medium sauté pan, heat the oil, parsley, garlic, and hot pepper (if using) on medium heat for 2 minutes.

Add the shrimp and salt. Continue cooking for about 3 minutes while mixing all the ingredients. The shrimp should be a light pink color.

Using a vegetable mill, purée the tomatoes. Add the puréed tomatoes to the pan and continue to cook on medium heat for 16 to 18 minutes.

In a separate pot, bring water to a boil. Add pasta and cook according to directions on package. Drain well.

Return the drained pasta to the empty pot and ladle sauce into the pot. Mix well on medium-high until the sauce fully coats the pasta.

Serve immediately.

Serves 4

3 pounds cockles or 4 dozen little-neck clams

8 garlic cloves

½ cup extra virgin olive oil

½ cup fresh parsley, chopped

1 hot cherry pepper, optional

½ cup white wine

1 14-ounce can cherry tomatoes

1 pint fresh cherry tomatoes, washed and cut in halves

1 pound pasta (linguine or spaghetti)

Sugo di Vongole con Pomodorini

Clam Sauce with Cherry Tomatoes

I make this recipe during the summer after a beautiful day at the beach. I buy the clams at the local markets out east on Long Island. This recipe can be made with either cockles or littleneck clams.

Wash the clams well, removing any sand. Pat dry with a paper towel.

In a medium sauté pan, add garlic, oil, ¼ cup parsley, and hot pepper (if using). Carefully sauté for about 2 minutes on high heat, making sure the garlic does not brown. Remove the garlic and set aside.

Add the clams and remaining ¼ cup parsley and continue cooking on medium-high heat for about 2 minutes. Add the wine and continue cooking for 3 to 4 minutes. Then add all tomatoes, re-add the garlic, and continue cooking for 10 to 12 minutes on medium high-heat. Discard any clams that are not open.

In a separate pot, bring water to a boil. Add pasta and cook according to directions on package. Drain well.

Return the drained pasta to the empty pot and ladle the sauce into the pot. Mix well on medium-high heat until the sauce fully coats the pasta.

Remove and discard clam shells that are empty. Serve immediately.

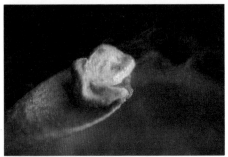

Serves 6

1 pound frozen porcini mushrooms, defrosted

½ cup extra virgin olive oil

½ cup fresh parsley, chopped

4 garlic cloves

1 small red hot pepper, optional

½ teaspoon sea salt

2 28-ounce cans Italian whole peeled tomatoes

1½ pounds pasta (pappardelle, tagliatelle, or mafalde)

Freshly grated cheese (Parmigiano Reggiano or Grana Padano), for serving

Sugo di Funghi Porcini

Porcini Mushroom Sauce

The unique flavor of porcini mushrooms makes for a quick and easy sauce that my family loves. This sauce can be served with many cuts of pasta. However, my favorite cuts are pappardelle, tagliatelle, or mafalde.

Rinse the mushrooms in cold water, pat dry with a paper towel, and slice horizontally into 2 to 3 slices per mushroom.

In a medium pan, sauté the oil, parsley, garlic, and hot pepper (if using) on medium heat for about 2 minutes.

Add the mushrooms and salt and continue to cook for about 3 minutes, stirring occasionally. Reduce heat slightly and continue to simmer for 5 minutes.

Using a vegetable mill, purée the tomatoes. Raise the heat to medium-high, add the puréed tomatoes, and continue cooking for another 5 minutes. Reduce the heat to a low simmer and cook uncovered for about 35 minutes.

In a separate pot, bring water to a boil. Add pasta and cook according to directions on package. Drain well.

Return the drained pasta to the empty pot and ladle sauce into the pot. Mix well on until the sauce fully coats the pasta.

Serve immediately with freshly grated cheese.

1 26-ounce bottle passata di pomodoro

2 garlic cloves

1 tablespoon hot pepper paste or ½
teaspoon crushed red chili pepper
flakes

¼ teaspoon sea salt

2 tablespoons extra virgin olive oil

Sugo Piccante per Pesce

Hot Sauce for Fish

This sauce is always made on Christmas Eve and is used as a dip-
ping sauce for the assorted fried fish.

Place the passata di pomodoro, garlic, pepper paste or crushed red pepper, salt, and oil in a medium saucepan. Cook on medium heat until the
sauce begins to boil.

Reduce heat and continue to cook on a low simmer for 10 to 12 minutes.

Remove and discard the garlic. Reheat if not immediately serving.

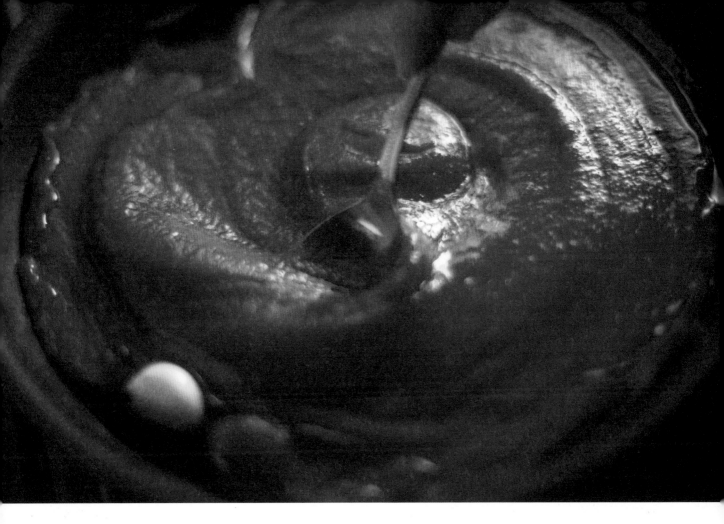

2 garlic cloves
¼ cup extra virgin olive oil
2 cups passata di pomodoro
¼ teaspoon sea salt

Sugo Finto

"Fake Sauce"

This sauce is usually used to flavor pasta that is mixed with a legume. This is not considered a real sauce because it cooks for about five minutes and the only seasoning is garlic. It is enough for nearly one pound of pasta.

In a medium-size frying pan, heat garlic and oil for 1 minute on medium heat.

Add passata di pomodoro and salt. Reduce heat to low and continue cooking for 5 minutes.

Remove and discard garlic. Reheat if not immediately serving.

Serves 4 to 5

1 head broccoli

2 teaspoons sea salt

1 pound pasta (fusilli, ziti, or penne rigate)

¼ cup extra virgin olive oil, plus more for serving

½ cup freshly grated cheese (Parmigiano Reggiano, Grana Padano, or Pecorino Romano), plus more for serving

Pasta con Broccoli

Pasta with Broccoli

This is a weekly staple meal for my family. The secret to this recipe is cooking fresh broccoli with the pasta. The stalks should be firm and the florets should be tight. My favorite pasta for this recipe is fusilli, although my mother often made this dish with broken linguine.

Wash the broccoli and remove and discard ¼-inch of the stem. Peel the stem, then cut off the remaining stem and slice into ½-inch pieces. Cut each broccoli spear in half.

Bring 4 quarts of cold water to a boil and add broccoli spears, stem, and salt. Return to a boil.

Add pasta, mix well, and continue cooking uncovered on medium-heat, stirring occasionally. Cook pasta according to directions on package.

Drain pasta and broccoli in a colander and reserve ¾ cup of pasta water.

Return the pasta and broccoli to the pot and mix in the pasta water, oil, and grated cheese. Cook on medium heat for 2 minutes, stirring continuously.

Serve immediately with additional oil and freshly grated cheese to taste.

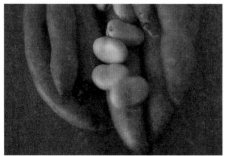

Serves 6

Fava and Peas with Pancetta recipe (see page 226)

½ pound pasta (tubettini or small shells)

2 tablespoons extra virgin olive oil, plus more for serving

¼ cup freshly grated cheese (Parmigiano Reggiano, Grana Padano, or Pecorino Romano), for serving

Pasta con Fave e Piselli

Pasta with Fava and Peas

This recipe reminds me of my late uncle and aunt, Zio Rocco and Zia Rosina. Zio Rocco was my mother's brother and an amazing cook. He loved to cook for his family and friends, and he often made this dish.

Prepare Fava and Peas with Pancetta according to recipe. Set aside.

In a separate pot, bring water to a boil. Add pasta and cook according to directions on package. Drain well.

On medium-high heat, reheat the Fava and Peas with Pancetta. Add the drained pasta, oil, and grated cheese. Mix well and continue cooking for about 2 minutes.

Let sit for about 10 minutes before serving with additional oil and freshly grated cheese to taste.

Serves 6

Chickpeas recipe (see page 75)
"Fake Sauce" (see page 107)
¾ pound pasta (tubetti or ditali)
Extra virgin olive oil, for serving
Freshly grated cheese (Parmigiano Reggiano, Grana Padano, or Pecorino Romano), for serving

Pasta con Ceci
Pasta and Chickpeas

This is a very simple dish to make. The secret to this dish is the "Fake Sauce," or Sugo Finto, which flavors the pasta. My favorite pasta shape with this recipe is tubetti or ditalini, but broken tagliatelle or broken pappardelle also work well.

Prepare Chickpeas according to recipe. Set aside.

Prepare "Fake Sauce" according to recipe. Set aside.

In a separate pot, bring water to a boil. Add pasta and cook according to directions on package. Drain well.

Return the pasta to the pot, add the sauce, and heat for 1 to 2 minutes, stirring continuously.

Add the chickpeas, mix well, and continue cooking on medium heat for 3 to 4 minutes.

Let sit for about 5 minutes before serving with oil and freshly grated cheese.

Serves 4 to 5

1½ pounds flat string beans (preferably Italian)

2 tomatoes, seeded, cored, and cut in halves

1 small onion, sliced

1 tablespoon sea salt

10 fresh basil leaves, chopped

1 medium Yukon potato, peeled and cut into quarters

½ pound pasta (broken bucatini or broken spaghetti)

2 tablespoons extra virgin olive oil, plus more for serving

¼ cup freshly grated cheese (Parmigiano Reggiano, Grana Padano, or Pecorino Romano), plus more for serving

Pasta con Fagiolini e Patate

Pasta with String Beans and Potatoes

This is another one of my favorite summer recipes. This recipe should be made when string beans are in peak season and most flavorful. We always grew string beans in our garden during the summer. The plants would grow to four or five feet tall, held up by a pole or stick. Each morning my mother would go into the garden to pick the string beans. When she had collected enough beans, this recipe would be prepared.

Wash string beans and remove and discard the stems. Cut each string bean in half, rewash, and place in a colander. Set aside.

In a pot with 3 quarts of cold water, place tomatoes, onion, salt, and basil and bring to a boil.

Add the string beans and continue cooking on medium heat until a boil is reached.

Reduce the heat to medium-low and cook semi-covered for about 25 minutes.

Add the potatoes and pasta to the pot and mix well. Raise heat to medium-high and continue cooking semi-covered, until al dente or about 12 minutes. Stir occasionally.

Drain pasta, string beans, and potatoes in a colander and reserve about 1 cup of pasta water.

Return the drained pasta, string beans, potatoes, and reserved water to the pot. Add the oil and grated cheese, mix well, and continue to cook an additional 1 to 2 minutes on medium heat.

Serve immediately with additional oil and freshly grated cheese to taste.

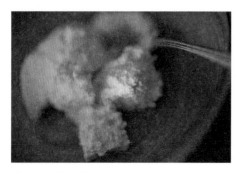

Pasta con Ricotta

Pasta with Ricotta

This recipe is so simple to make. Prep and cooking time is about five minutes total. This recipe works best with capellini or angel hair pasta.

Serves 1 to 2

1 teaspoon extra virgin olive oil

2 heaping tablespoons fresh ricotta cheese

3 ounces pasta, broken in half (capellini or angel hair)

In a bowl, add the oil and ricotta. Mix well.

In a separate pot, bring water to a boil. Add pasta and cook according to directions on package.

When the pasta is cooked, remove with a tong, and place in the bowl with the ricotta and oil. Mix well, adding pasta water if too dry.

Serve immediately.

Serves 1

4 ounces of Acini di Pepe or another small pasta shape

1 tablespoon salted butter

1/3 cup freshly grated cheese (Parmigiana Reggiano or Grana Padano)

1 large egg

Pastina con Uovo, Burro e Formaggio

Pastina with Egg, Butter and Cheese

Sometimes called "Italian Penicillin," this simple and hearty pastina dish became a staple in our house during winter months or cold and flu season. The trick is to use the precise amount of water since the pastina is not drained.

In a small pot, bring 3 cups of water to a boil. Add the pastina and cook according to directions on package. Once the pasta is cooked, turn off the heat. Do not drain the pastina.

In a small bowl, beat egg until frothy. Slowly add 2 tablespoons of pasta water and continue beating. (This step tempers the eggs to ensure it will not become scrambled when it is added to the pastina.)

Add the butter and grated cheese to the pot with the pastina and mix well.

Add the tempered egg mixture to the pastina pot and mix on medium-low for 3 to 4 minutes, stirring continuously.

Serve immediately.

Even More Pasta:

Fresh and Baked Pasta

Pasta Fatta a Mano (Filei Calabrese)
Hand-Rolled Pasta

Lasagna al Forno con Polpettine
Baked Lasagna with Tiny Meatballs

Anelletti al Forno con Carne Tritata e Piselli
Baked Anelletti with Chopped Meat and Peas

Pennoni al Forno con Funghi
Baked Pennoni with Mushrooms

Zitoni al Forno con Sugo di Maiale
Baked Zitoni with Pork Sauce

This third and smallest pasta chapter contains fresh and baked pastas. It includes the Pasta Fatta a Mano (Filei Calabrese), which I made with my mother as a young child. Baked pasta was served for large celebrations or special occasions so that there were no last-minute preparations when guests arrived and so that the kitchen would be clean.

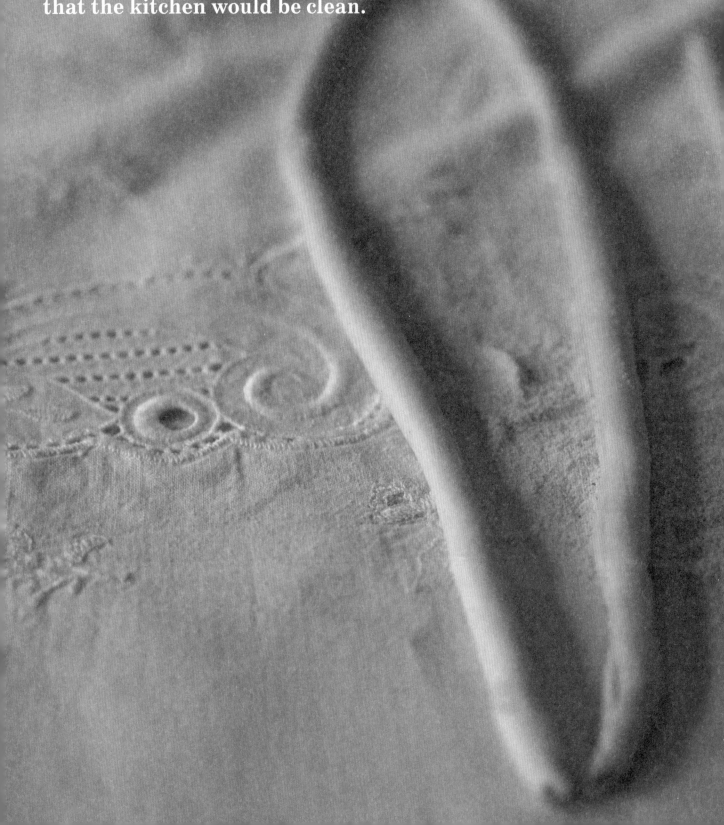

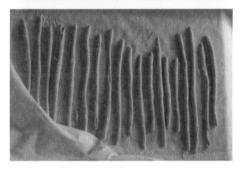

Serves 4 to 6 (makes about 1¾ pounds of dough)

1 Sunday Sauce with Meatballs and Sausage (see page 82)

3¼ cups 00 flour, sifted (17 ounces)

1¼ cup water

Pure olive oil, for greasing the mixing bowl and knitting needle

2 cotton or linen tablecloths or bed sheets, for rolling the pasta

Coarse semolina flour, to preventing sticking

1 long knitting needle or clothes hanger clipped

Freshly grated cheese (Parmigiano Reggiano, Grana Padano, or Pecorino Romano), for serving

½ tablespoon sea salt

Pasta Fatta a Mano (Filei Calabrese)
Hand-Rolled Pasta

While many people make homemade pasta, this dish is unique because each piece of pasta is hand-rolled. I remember waking up at five in the morning to make this recipe. We would make sure the entire family was coming over for dinner. This was another one of my Zio Rocco and Zia Rosina's signature dishes. This pasta works well with meat sauces. This homemade pasta is the fresh equivalent of dried Filei Calabrese.

Prepare Sunday Sauce with Meatballs recipe. Set aside.

In a mixing bowl, combine flour and water and knead well for 5 to 10 minutes until a smooth dough is formed. Oil a separate large bowl, place dough in the bowl, cover with a towel, and let sit for about 30 minutes.

Line a large table with the tablecloth or bed sheet. Generously sprinkle with coarse semolina flour to prevent the pasta from sticking. Place a second cloth or sheet on top of the first. (This second sheet will cover the pasta once it has been rolled.)

Lightly grease a knitting needle. Take a ¾-ounce piece of dough and roll it into a 1-inch log. Place on the needle and continue to roll until it has reached about 6 inches in length. Gently slide the dough off the needle. Place on the table and cover with cloth or sheet.

Continue the above step until all of the dough has been formed into pasta. Re-oil the needle in between every few pieces of pasta.

Let pasta dry covered for at least 2 hours before cooking.

When preparing to serve dinner, reheat the sauce and remove the meatballs and sausage (to be served as a secondo piatto to the pasta).

Bring a large pot of cold water to a boil and then add pasta and salt. Make sure the pasta is generously covered by water. Cook until al dente or 20 to 30 minutes. Drain well.

Return drained pasta to the pot and ladle sauce into the pot. Mix well on medium-high until the sauce fully coats the pasta.

Serve immediately with freshly grated cheese.

Serves 8 to 10

Pork Sauce with Meatballs and Sausage (see page 84) (preferably mini meatballs)

1½ pounds pasta (dry lasagna)

1½ pounds mozzarella cheese, shredded (or a combination of shredded mozzarella, Italian Asiago, and Italian Fontina cheese)

1 pound fresh ricotta cheese

1 tablespoon freshly grated cheese (Parmigiano Reggiano, Grana Padano, or Pecorino Romano)

Lasagna al Forno con Polpettine

Baked Lasagna with Tiny Meatballs

There are only three recipes in this book that I consider difficult, and this is one of them. Many may claim that precooked lasagna sheets work just as well as regular lasagna sheets, but I disagree. One of my pasta suppliers taught me a trick that makes this recipe easier. Instead of boiling all the lasagna sheets at once, I boil the sheets in batches. I only boil the number of pieces needed for each layer. When they are cooked, I remove them with a tong and place them around a colander (hanging off the side so they do not stick). Using the same salted boiling water, I begin the next batch. Lasagna is always made for Christmas Day dinner or special occasions.

Prepare Pork Sauce with Meatballs and Sausage according to recipe. Make sure the meatballs are mini in size.

Remove most of the sausage and some of the pork meat from sauce and place in a dish. Shred the pork meat and crumble the sausage with a fork. Mix together and set aside.

With a slotted spoon, remove meatballs from sauce. Set aside.

Preheat the oven to 400°F.

Cook lasagna sheets according to the directions on package or until the lasagna is tender. (I boil the lasagna in batches, remove each piece with a tong when tender, and place around the rim of a colander.)

To assemble the lasagna:

1. In a deep, rectangular baking dish (14.5-by-11-by-3 inches), add 2 cups of sauce.
2. Evenly layer the below ingredients:
    a. Cooked lasagna sheets
    b. 1½ cups shredded mozzarella
    c. 3 heaping tablespoons ricotta
    d. 1 ladle crumbled meat mixture
    e. 1½ ladles meatballs
    f. 1 cup sauce
3. Repeat the above steps 2 more times.
4. Top the last layer with cooked lasagna sheets, 2½ cups of sauce, remaining shredded mozzarella, and grated cheese.

Cover the entire dish with aluminum foil. Bake in the oven for 1 hour, rotating the dish after 30 minutes.

Let sit for at least 1 hour before serving.

Notes:

- Lasagna bakes much better in a baking dish than in a disposable pan.

- Instead of mini meatballs, standard meatballs can be made and then crumbled with a fork.

- There will be some remaining pork meat, sausage, and sauce that can be frozen and used as a base for a quick sauce.

Serves 6

½ cup extra virgin olive oil

1 medium onion, chopped

2 garlic cloves

1 pound ground meat (beef or pork)

1 teaspoon sea salt

39 ounces passata di pomodoro (1½ bottles)

1 cup frozen peas, rinsed and drained in colander, optional

Pure olive oil, for greasing

¼ cup breadcrumbs

1 pound pasta (anelletti)

1 pound primo sale or mozzarella cheese, cubed

½ cup freshly grated cheese (Parmigiano Reggiano or Grana Padano)

Anelletti al Forno con Carne Tritata e Piselli

Baked Anelletti with Chopped Meat and Peas

This is one of my son's favorite dishes and a typical dish made in Palermo, Sicily. There are different variations. It can be made with cubed fried eggplant instead of chopped meat and peas. It is a very easy and quick baked pasta dish to prepare.

Preheat the oven to 375°F.

In a medium sauté pan, add extra virgin olive oil, onion, and garlic and heat on medium heat for 3 to 4 minutes.

Add the ground meat and salt and mix well. Continue to cook until the ground meat is pink in color, about 4 to 5 minutes.

Add passata di pomodoro and ½ cup of water and continue cooking on medium heat for 10 minutes.

Add the peas and continue cooking semi-covered for 8 to 10 minutes.

Remove and discard the garlic.

Lightly grease a deep, rectangular baking dish (14.5-by-11-by-3 or 9-by-13-by-2 inches) with pure olive oil and then spread a thin layer of breadcrumbs along the bottom of the dish.

In a separate pot, bring water to a boil. Add pasta and cook according to directions on package. Drain well.

In a large bowl, combine the pasta, cubed cheese, and grated cheese and mix well. Add the sauce and continue mixing.

Place the above mixture in the baking dish and top with additional breadcrumbs. Cover the dish with aluminum foil and bake for about 35 minutes.

Let sit for about 1 hour before serving.

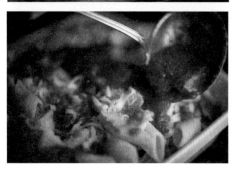

Serves 8

Pork Sauce with Meatballs and Sausage (see page 84)

2 pounds pasta (pennoni rigate or rigatoni)

1½ pounds mozzarella cheese, shredded

8 ounces white button mushrooms, thinly sliced

2 tablespoons freshly grated cheese (Parmigiano Reggiano, Grana Padano, or Pecorino Romano)

Pennoni al Forno con Funghi

Baked Pennoni with Mushrooms

I learned how to make this pasta dish from my mother-in-law. The mushrooms are added fresh and do not need any prior cooking. It is much simpler to prepare than a lasagna since there are no pasta sheets to separate after boiling. Rigatoni pasta also works if pennoni is not available.

Prepare Pork Sauce with Meatballs and Sausage recipe.

Remove pork meat, sausage, and meatballs from sauce and set aside (to serve as a secondo piatto to the pasta).

When the sauce is ready, preheat the oven to 400°F.

In a separate pot, bring water to a boil. Add pasta and cook according to directions on package. Drain well.

In a deep, rectangular baking dish (14.5-by-11-by-3 inches), add 2 cups of sauce.

Add a layer of cooked pasta, a thin layer of mozzarella, and a layer of mushrooms. Top with 1½ cups of sauce and repeat layering 2 additional times.

Top the last layer with remaining pasta, mozzarella, mushrooms, grated cheese, and 2 cups of sauce.

Cover the dish with aluminum foil. Bake for 45 to 55 minutes or until the mozzarella is bubbling.

Let sit for at least 1 hour before serving.

Serves 6 to 8

Pork Sauce with Meatballs and Sausage (see page 84)

2 pounds pasta (long zitoni or long candele)

¾ pound Italian fontina cheese, shredded

½ pound mozzarella cheese, shredded

3 tablespoons freshly grated cheese (Parmigiano Reggiano, Grana Padano, or Pecorino Romano)

Zitoni al Forno con Sugo di Maiale

Baked Zitoni with Pork Sauce

When my children were little, I always hosted large birthday parties for them. Although we would cater some of the food, my mother would never allow me to order pasta. This is my family's favorite party pasta. We would prepare it early in the morning and bake it a few hours before it was to be served. Zitoni pasta is sold in different lengths, either 25- or 50-centimeters long. I prefer the shorter pasta because it is not necessary to cut in order to fit it into the pot. Long candele pasta can also work for this dish.

Prepare Pork Sauce with Meatballs and Sausage recipe. Set aside.

When the sauce is ready, preheat the oven to 400°F.

In a separate bowl, mix the shredded fontina and mozzarella.

Remove 4 links of sausages, crumble with a fork, and set aside. Remove about half of the pork meat, shred with a fork, and set aside. Remove the meatballs and any remaining sausage and pork meat from the sauce and set aside (to be served as a secondo piatto to the pasta).

In a separate pot, bring water to a boil. Add pasta and cook according to directions on package. Drain well.

In a deep, rectangular baking dish (14.5-by-11-by-3 inches), place 2 cups of sauce. Then place a single layer of the pasta and scatter the crumbled sausage and shredded meat. Top with a thin layer of the shredded cheeses, 1 tablespoon grated cheese, and 1 cup of sauce. Repeat layering 2 additional times.

Cover the dish with aluminum foil. Bake for 50 to 60 minutes.

Let sit for at least 1 hour before serving.

Note: If Italian fontina cheese is not available, substitute with Italian Asiago.

Rice
and Polenta

Polenta con Broccoli e Finocchio
Polenta with Broccoli and Fennel

Riso Bianco
Simple White Rice

Riso con Carne Tritata e Piselli
Rice with Chopped Meat and Peas

Riso con Zucchine e Carote
Rice with Zucchini and Carrots

The Calabrese make riso using a completely different method of cooking. The rice isn't toasted or simmered with bouillon or stock, as a risotto would be. Rather, it's boiled in a perfect amount of water and, when fully cooked, served with either extra virgin olive oil and Parmigiano cheese or sautéed vegetables or meat stirred in. Sometimes vegetables are cooked along with the water to flavor the dish.

Polenta was traditionally prepared in the winter, and strictly by one method—like a porridge with broccoli and fennel. Pieces of pork fat were often added at the end of cooking. Today, I use instant polenta, which is cornmeal ground to a very fine consistency. It cooks in a few minutes and doesn't require the patience and constant stirring that regular polenta requires. In my opinion, there is not enough difference in flavor to justify the extra work.

Serves 4 to 6

1 head broccoli

2 bulbs fennel with leaves and stem

2 teaspoons sea salt

1½ cups instant polenta

Pork fat or extra virgin olive oil, for serving

Freshly grated cheese (Parmigiano Reggiano or Grana Padano), for serving

Polenta con Broccoli e Finocchio

Polenta with Broccoli and Fennel

Known as frascatule in Calabrese, this combination of vegetables, polenta, and pork fat creates a truly unique dish. This dish was always made in the winter months. While it is primarily served as a primo piatto instead of pasta, it is also a wonderful accompaniment to grilled meats.

Wash the broccoli and remove and discard ¼-inch of the stem. Peel the stem, then cut off the remaining stem and slice into ½-inch pieces. Cut each broccoli spear in half.

Wash the fennel and cut the leaves and stems into ½-inch slices.

In a large pot with 3¾ quarts of cold water, place broccoli, fennel, and salt and bring to a boil. Continue cooking over medium-high heat, uncovered for about 15 minutes.

Slowly add the polenta, stirring continuously. Continue cooking, stirring about every 30 seconds, over medium-low heat for about 5 minutes.

Let sit for a few minutes before serving with oil or pork fat and freshly grated cheese.

Riso Bianco
Simple White Rice

Riso bianco is a simple rice dish served plain or as a side dish for veal stew or oven-baked chicken. According to my mother, white rice also has medicinal value. When I was a young child and didn't feel well, my mother put boiled rice into plastic bags to create hot packs. She placed these packs on my back to alleviate any colds or respiratory issues.

In a large pot, bring 7 cups of water to a boil. Add rice and salt and return to a boil.

Continue cooking uncovered on a low simmer, occasionally stirring, for 16 to 18 minutes or until the rice is tender.

Let sit for 5 minutes before serving with oil and freshly grated cheese.

Serves 4

2 cups Arborio rice (1 pound)
1½ teaspoons sea salt
Extra virgin olive oil, for serving
Freshly grated cheese (Parmigiano Reggiano or Grana Padano), for serving

Serves 4 to 6

Sauce:

1 small onion, sliced

¼ cup extra virgin olive oil

3 fresh basil leaves, chopped

1 garlic clove

¾ pound ground beef

½ teaspoon sea salt

2 cups passata di pomodoro

Rice:

1½ teaspoon sea salt

1 small onion, sliced

1 cup frozen peas, rinsed in cold water

2 cups Arborio rice (1 pound)

2 tablespoons freshly grated cheese (Parmigiana Reggiano, Grana Padano, or Pecorino Romano), plus more for serving

Riso con Carne Tritata e Piselli

Rice with Chopped Meat and Peas

This is one of my husband's favorite dishes that his mother always made for him. It is a simple dish that is served as a primo piatto, instead of pasta. It is very hearty and often made in the winter months. This dish tastes like the inside of a Sicilian arancini!

In a medium sauté pan, add the onion, oil, basil, and garlic and sauté for about 2 minutes. Add the ground meat and salt and mash the meat with a fork while mixing all the ingredients. Continue cooking on medium heat for 4 to 5 minutes or until all the meat is browned.

Add the passata di pomodoro and continue to cook for an additional 10 minutes. Set aside.

In a separate pot, place 6 cups of water, salt, onion, and peas and bring to a boil. Add rice and continue cooking for about 15 minutes, stirring constantly.

Add the sauce to the rice pot and cook for about 3 minutes, constantly stirring and mixing all the ingredients. Add cheese and mix well.

Let sit for about 10 minutes completely covered before serving with additional freshly grated cheese to taste.

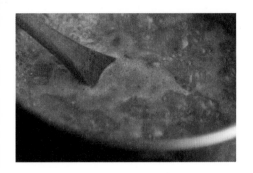

Riso con Zucchine e Carote
Rice with Zucchini and Carrots

This recipe is the Calabrese version of vegetable risotto. It can be served as a side dish to grilled meats and chicken.

Serves 4 to 6

1 medium onion, sliced

1 large carrot

1 medium zucchini

2 teaspoons sea salt

2 cups Arborio rice (1 pound)

2 tablespoons extra virgin olive oil

¼ cup freshly grated cheese (Parmigiano Reggiano or Grana Padano)

Wash and peel the carrot. Wash the zucchini. Grate carrot and zucchini using the coarse side of a box grater.

In a large pot with 7½ cups of cold water, add the onion, carrot, zucchini, and salt and bring to a boil.

Add the rice and continue to cook on medium heat, stirring frequently until a boil is reached.

Reduce the heat slightly and continue to cook for about 16 minutes, stirring frequently to make sure the rice does not stick to the bottom. Add freshly grated cheese and oil to taste, mix well.

Let sit for about 5 minutes before serving.

Eggs

Uova Affogate con Olio e Origano
Poached Eggs with Oil and Oregano

Uova con Cipolle e Ricotta
Eggs with Onions and Ricotta

Frittata con Asparagi
Asparagus Frittata

Uova con Soppressata e Olive
Eggs with Soppressata and Olives

Uova con Salami 'Nduja
Eggs with 'Nduja Salami

My mother always bought fresh eggs at LaPera Bros. Poultry. When she cracked an egg, if the yolk wasn't firm, she discarded the egg as that meant it wasn't fresh. At breakfast, we ate them poached along with a cup of coffee and a few biscuits. For lunch or weekend brunch, my mother served eggs cooked with salami, sauce, and olives.

The dishes in this section include a variety of both light and substantial egg dishes that can offer either a quick breakfast or hearty brunch. The versatility of eggs is remarkable; each time you add an ingredient to an egg dish, it takes on a completely new taste and texture.

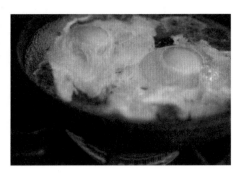

Serves 1

2 large eggs

⅛ teaspoon sea salt, for seasoning

1 teaspoon extra virgin olive oil, for seasoning

Dry Italian oregano, for seasoning

Uova Affogate con Olio e Origano

Poached Eggs with and Oil and Oregano

This is a very simple and healthy breakfast meal. I poach the eggs and use olive oil instead of butter as a topping. It was my mom's favorite breakfast. I would often find her sitting in her kitchen most mornings, enjoying this with friselle and a cup of coffee.

In an 8-inch frying pan, bring 1½ cups of water to a boil. Crack both eggs into the boiling water.

Continue cooking on medium heat, spooning some of the water on top of the yolks. Cook for 2 to 2½ minutes or until the eggs are cooked to your liking.

Season with salt, oil, and oregano to taste. Serve immediately.

Serves 1

3 tablespoons extra virgin olive oil

2 scallions, thinly sliced

½ cup passata di pomodoro

Pinch of sea salt

2 large eggs

2 heaping tablespoons fresh ricotta cheese

Uova con Cipolla e Ricotta

Eggs with Onions and Ricotta

This is my mother-in-law's take on weekend brunch.

In a medium nonstick frying pan, add the oil and scallions and sauté on medium heat for about 2 minutes.

Add the passata di pomodoro and salt and continue to cook for about 2 minutes.

Crack both eggs into the pan and cover with a lid. Cook for 2 to 4 minutes or until the eggs are cooked to your liking.

Place a heaping tablespoon of ricotta on each side of the eggs in the pan and let sit completely covered for about 1 minute.

With a spatula, gently remove the eggs and ricotta and place on a dish. Top with the remaining sauce in the pan.

Serve immediately.

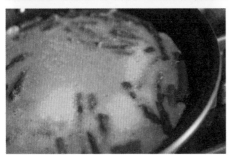

Serves 2

Boiled Asparagus (see page 218)

4 large eggs, at room temperature

2 tablespoons freshly grated cheese (Parmigiana Reggiano, Grana Pada-no, or Pecorino Romano)

2 grinds freshly ground black pep-per

Pinch of sea salt

2 tablespoons pure olive oil

Frittata con Asparagi

Asparagus Frittata

I always boil extra asparagus so I can make this frittata with the leftovers. I learned from a friend that you should always use room temperature eggs when making this dish.

Cut the boiled asparagus stalks into small pieces about 1-inch long.

Whisk the eggs, cheese, pepper, and salt until frothy.

In an 8-inch nonstick frying pan, place the oil and asparagus and cook on medium heat for 1 to 2 minutes or until the oil begins to sizzle.

Reduce heat to medium-low, add the egg mixture, and let the mixture cook (without mixing or stirring the eggs). As the eggs begin to set, lift the edges to let the liquid from the top flow underneath. Cook for 8 to 12 minutes or until the bottom is golden brown and minimal liquid remains on top.

Cover the pan with a flat plate and flip the frittata onto the plate. Slide the uncooked side back into the pan and continue cooking for 3 to 4 minutes or until golden brown on the bottom.

Serve immediately.

147

Eggs with Soppressata and Olives

This recipe is often made for a weekend brunch. I call it breakfast "Calabrese style." It is usually accompanied by Italian bread or friselle to dip into the egg.

In a medium nonstick frying pan, add the oil, soppressata, and olives and begin to cook on medium heat for 1 to 2 minutes.

Stir in the passata di pomodoro. When the passata begins to sizzle, crack the eggs into the pan and cook for about 1 minute. Cover the pan and continue cooking on medium-low for 2 to 4 minutes or until the eggs are cooked to your liking.

Serve immediately.

Serves 1 to 2

¼ cup extra virgin olive oil

5 slices hot soppressata, hand-cut

10 olives (Calabrese, Gaeta, or Dry-Cured), with pits

½ cup passata di pomodoro

3 large eggs

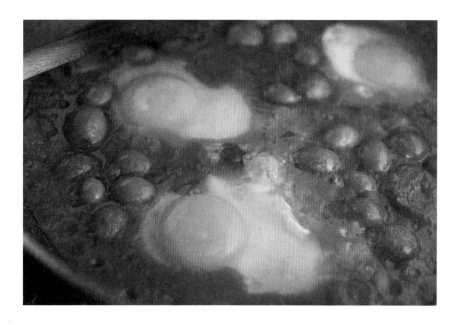

149

Uova con Salame 'Nduja

Eggs with 'Nduja Salami

Spilinga, a small town in Calabria, is famous for this spicy spreadable salami, known as 'nduja. This salami works great paired with eggs.

In a medium nonstick pan, add the oil and passata di pomodoro and cook on medium heat for about 2 minutes, stirring occasionally.

Add the 'nduja and continue cooking on medium heat for 1 to 2 minutes, smashing the 'nduja with a fork.

Crack both eggs into the mixture, place the lid on the pan, and continue cooking on low heat until the eggs are cooked to your liking.

Serve immediately.

Serves 1

1 tablespoon extra virgin olive oil
½ cup passata di pomodoro
4 slices of 'nduja salami, hand-cut
2 large eggs

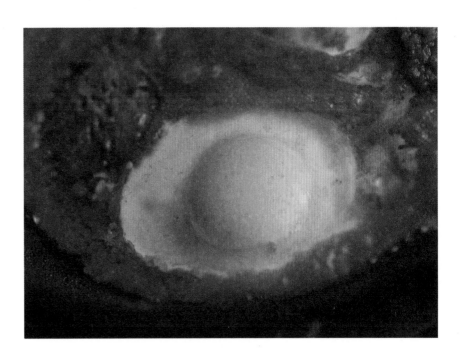

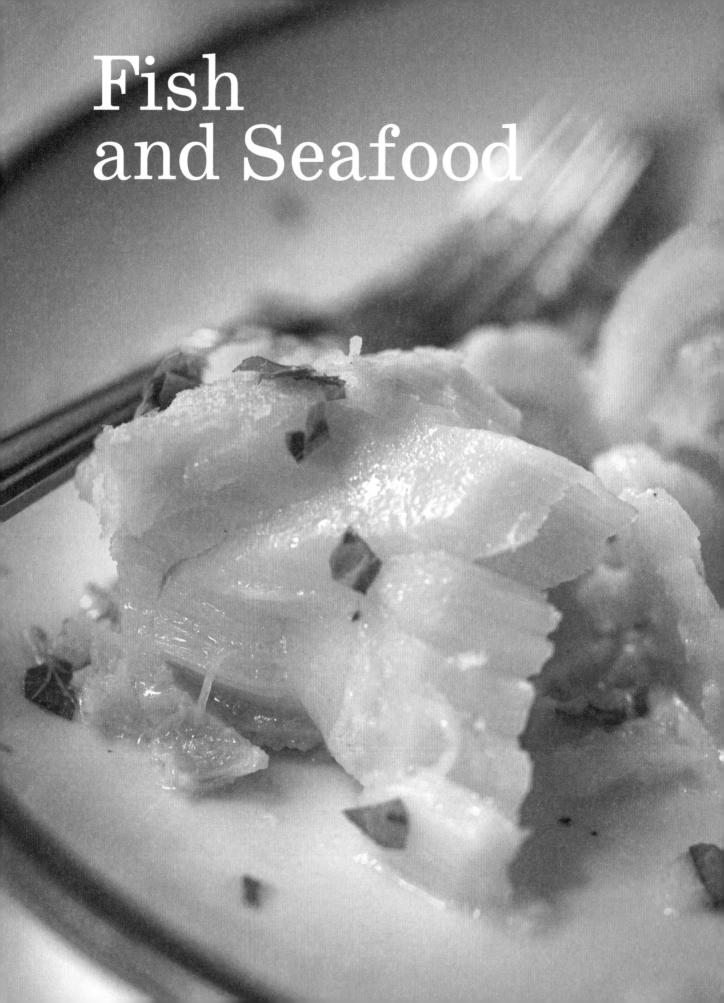

Fish
and Seafood

Pesce Halibut Affogato con Aglio e Pomodoro

Poached Halibut with Garlic and Tomato

Baccalà Fritto

Fried Baccalà

Baccalà con Patate, Pomodori Secchi e Olive

Baccalà with Potatoes, Sun-Dried Tomatoes, and Olives

Calamari Fritti con Salsa Piccante

Fried Calamari with Hot Sauce

Frittura Mista di Pesce

Mixed Fish Fry

Pesce Spada al Forno con Pomodoro e Prezzemolo

Baked Swordfish with Tomato and Parsley

When my parents lived in Calabria, meat was never eaten on Wednesdays or Fridays. This tradition was continued in America. The type of fish that was served depended on what was fresh and in season. On Fridays in October, November, and December, we would make either baccalà or stoccafisso, two varieties of preserved codfish. As a child, I always found it difficult to tell the difference between them. I knew they each had a distinctive taste but was confused as to which was which. When I asked my mom, she would reply, "stocco è stocco e baccalà è baccalà." She could not understand how I could not tell them apart. To her, it was as obvious as the difference between an apple and a pear. As I grew older, I learned that stocco was air-cured cod and baccalà was salt-cured cod.

Meat was never eaten on Christmas Eve or New Year's Eve. The meals on these nights were virtually identical and my mother made thirteen different dishes. At about eleven at night, after fruit and coffee had been served, she would begin frying zeppole. Today, my Americanized family celebrates with seven seafood dishes on the night before Christmas.

Although my family often ate fish due to tradition, today I serve it as a healthy alternative to beef and pork. In addition to being high in protein, it is often lower in both saturated fat and cholesterol. Additionally, much of the unsaturated fats in fish have been proven to be healthy for the heart.

Serves 2 to 3

1 halibut steak, cut in half (about 2 pounds)

2 plum tomatoes, cut into quarters, seeded, and cored

10 sprigs fresh parsley, chopped, plus more for serving

½ teaspoon sea salt

3 tablespoons extra virgin olive oil

4 garlic cloves

Pesce Halibut Affogato con Aglio e Pomodoro

Poached Halibut Fish with Garlic and Tomato

Halibut is very high in protein and low in fat. Prepared in this simple manner, you have a very healthy meal. The key to this recipe is the right amount of water. By the time the fish has cooked, most of the water should have evaporated.

Wash the halibut in cold water. Pat dry with a paper towel.

In a pan that fits the fish in a single layer, add 2 cups of water, tomatoes, parsley, salt, oil, and garlic. Bring to a boil.

Add the halibut and continue to cook on medium heat for 5 minutes. Gently flip the fish and continue to cook for another 8 minutes. Flip the fish again and cook for an either an additional 4 minutes, until the fish is cooked through, or until an internal temperature of 140 to 145°F is reached. During this cooking time, occasionally spoon the cooking water over the fish and move the fish in the pan, making sure it does not stick to the bottom.

Let sit for 5 minutes before serving with any remaining liquid from the pan.

Note: Cooking time will vary depending on the size of the fish. Water will vary depending on the size of the pan.

Serves 4 to 6

2 pounds boneless baccalà

1½ cups unbleached all-purpose flour, for dredging

3 cups pure olive oil, for frying

1 lemon, cut into wedges, for serving

Sea salt, for serving

Baccalà Fritto

Fried Baccalà

Fried Baccalà (salt-cured cod fish) was usually served for lunch when baked Baccalà with Potatoes, Sun-Dried Tomatoes, and Olives was being made for dinner. I usually place the pot with the soaking baccalà in the refrigerator so there is no smell of soaking fish lingering in the kitchen. At times, I soak enough baccalà for two dinners and then freeze the extra soaked fish for two to three weeks.

To soak the baccalà:

Cut the baccalà into 3-inch pieces and then place in a large pot or plastic tub filled with cold water. Let sit for 5 minutes and replace with fresh water. Place the pot under the faucet and let cold water run on a slow drip for about 2 hours.

Remove the pot from under the faucet and place the water-filled pot containing the fish in the refrigerator. Each morning and evening, replace the water with fresh cold water.

The baccalà needs to soak for 2½ to 3 days, depending on the dryness and thickness of the fish. To check the saltiness, cut a little piece and boil it for 1 minute and then taste. If too salty, soak for an additional 1 to 2 days.

To fry the baccalà:

Pat dry the soaked baccalà with a paper towel. Dredge in flour and set aside.

In a 12-inch pan, add oil (about ½-inch in depth) and heat for a few minutes on medium heat. To test the oil, place a pinch of the baccalà coating in the oil; if the oil begins to sizzle, the oil is ready. Add the baccalà in a single layer. Reduce the heat slightly and fry until golden brown in color on both sides. Remove from the pan and place on a paper towel-lined dish to absorb excess oil.

Season with salt. Serve warm with lemon wedges on the side.

Serves 6

Fried Baccalà (see page 159)

2 large Yukon potatoes, peeled and cut into quarters

½ teaspoon sea salt

10 pieces sun-dried tomatoes

4 dried cherry peppers or 2 fresh red round hot peppers

2 tablespoons hot or sweet pepper paste, optional

⅓ cup extra virgin olive oil

2 large onions, sliced

2 garlic cloves

½ cup Calabrese or Gaeta olives

1 28-ounce can Italian whole peeled tomatoes

Baccalà con Patate, Pomodori Secchi e Olive

Baccalà with Potatoes, Sun-Dried Tomatoes, and Olives

This is another one of my signature dishes. We eat baccalà on Fridays from in October until mid-January. This was always served on Christmas Eve and New Year's Eve. This dish can be prepared in the morning and baked a few hours before dinner. You will need a few loaves of Italian bread for dipping—try the recipe and you will know why.

Prepare Fried Baccalà according to recipe. Set aside.

Place the potatoes in a bowl with warm water and ½ teaspoon salt. Set aside.

Place the sun-dried tomatoes (and dried peppers, if using) in a bowl with warm water for about 10 minutes. Remove from water and pat dry with a paper towel. Set aside.

In a sauté pan, add the pepper paste (if using), oil, onions, garlic, olives, sun-dried tomatoes, and peppers and sauté on medium heat for about 3 minutes or until the onion is softened. Set aside.

Preheat the oven to 375°F.

Using a vegetable mill, purée the canned tomatoes. In a large baking dish, place a thin layer of the puréed tomato. Then add the fried baccalà and potatoes in a single layer. Top with the sautéed mixture, followed by the remaining puréed tomato. The baking dish should be large enough to fit the baccalà and potatoes in a single layer.

Baked completely covered for 45 to 60 minutes, rotating the pan occasionally in the oven. The dish can be removed when a fork easily pierces through the potatoes.

Let sit for about 20 minutes before serving.

Note: Cooking time will vary depending on thickness of baccalà.

Serves 4- 6

2 ½ pounds calamari tentacles and tubes

3 cups all purpose flour, sifted

Pure olive oil for frying

Sea salt

Lemon wedges

Hot Sauce recipe (see page 106)

Calamari Fritti con Salsa Piccante

Fried Calamari with Hot Sauce

Fried calamari are meant to be eaten right out of the pan. The secret to this recipe is getting the oil at the right temperature. I am not a fan of gadgets but a deep-frying thermometer will ensure the oil is at the right temperature. If the oil is too hot, the calamari will burn on the outside and not cook properly on the inside. If it is not hot enough, the calamari coating will never turn golden in color.

Cut the tubes into 1 inch rings. Then wash the tubes and tentacles in cold water, rinsing a few times. Pat dry with a paper towel.

In a bowl, add about 2 cups of flour and half the calamari. Mix, making sure the calamari are completely covered with the flour.

In a cast iron deep pot, add pure olive oil to fill about ½ the size of the pot (about 3 inches in depth). Heat on medium until the temperature reaches about 350–360°F.

Add the calamari in batches, placing them in a single layer in the pot. Continue to cook until golden brown. Remove and place on a paper towel lined dish to absorb excess oil. Season with sea salt to taste.

Serve immediately with lemon wedges and hot sauce on the side.

Note: The trick to the perfectly tender and crispy calamari is to not move them around in the oil once they've started frying.

Serves 10

1 pound sea scallops

1 pound large shrimp, cleaned and deveined

1 pound filet of sole

3 large eggs

4½ cups breadcrumbs, for coating

4 cups pure olive oil, for frying

Mixed Fish Fry

Mixed fish fry was always made on Christmas Eve. My children would always help me with this dish. They would bread the fish in the morning and then I would just need to fry it for a few hours before dinner. The different types of fish can either be fried individually or all together in batches. This recipe is typically served as a main course. I usually serve it as an appetizer with a hot sauce on the side for dipping.

Wash all of the fish and pat dry with a paper towel.

Cut each slice of sole into 4 pieces and each scallop into halves, if too large.

In a small bowl, beat the eggs. Dip each piece of fish in the egg and then in the breadcrumbs.

In a 13-inch pan, add oil (about ½-inch in depth) and heat for 3 to 4 minutes on medium heat. To test the oil, place a pinch of the fish coating in the oil; if the oil begins to sizzle, the oil is ready.

Add the fish in a single layer. Reduce the heat slightly and fry until golden brown in color on both sides. Remove and place on a paper-towel lined dish to absorb excess oil. If frying in batches, additional oil may be added to the pan if needed.

Serve warm or at room temperature. If desired, serve with Hot Sauce for Fish (see page 106).

Serves 4

2 pieces fresh swordfish (about 1½ pounds each)

Sea salt, for seasoning

Freshly ground black pepper, for seasoning

½ cup fresh parsley, chopped

⅓ cup pure olive oil

2 garlic cloves, cut in half

1 cup passata di pomodoro

Pesce Spada al Forno con Pomodoro e Prezzemolo

Baked Swordfish with Tomato and Parsley

Swordfish is another healthy fish that is high in protein and low in fat. This is a simple and easy recipe that is ready in under 1 hour. Always buy fresh swordfish, not frozen, and look for steaks that are bright in color.

Wash the swordfish and pat dry with a paper towel. Season the fish on both sides with salt and pepper.

Preheat the oven to 375°F.

In a baking dish (9-by-13-by-2 inches), combine the parsley, oil, garlic, and passata di pomodoro.

Place the fish on top of the mixture and bake uncovered for 15 minutes.

Remove from the oven, flip the fish with a spatula, and continue baking until the fish is cooked through, about 30 minutes or until an internal temperature of 140 to 145°F is reached.

Let sit for 5 minutes. To serve, pour remaining juices from the pan over the fish.

Note: The baking dish should be large enough to hold the fish in a single layer. Baking time may vary up to 10 minutes, depending on the thickness of the swordfish.

Meat

Polpette
Meatballs

Cotolette "Impanate" (Pollo, Vitello o Maiale)
Fried Cutlets (Chicken, Veal, or Pork)

Cotolette alla Parmigiana (Pollo, Vitello o Maiale)
Cutlets Parmigiana (Chicken, Veal,
or Pork)

Bistecca Rib-Eye con Peperoni e Pomodori
Rib-Eye Steak with Peppers and Tomatoes

Bistecca affettata con Funghi, Peperoni e Pomodori
Pepper Steak with Mushrooms,
Peppers, and Tomatoes

Spezzatino di Vitello con Salsiccia
Veal Stew with Sausage

Coniglio alla Cacciatora
Rabbit Cacciatore-Style

Trippa con Pomodoro, Patate e Piselli
Tripe with Tomato, Potatoes, and Peas

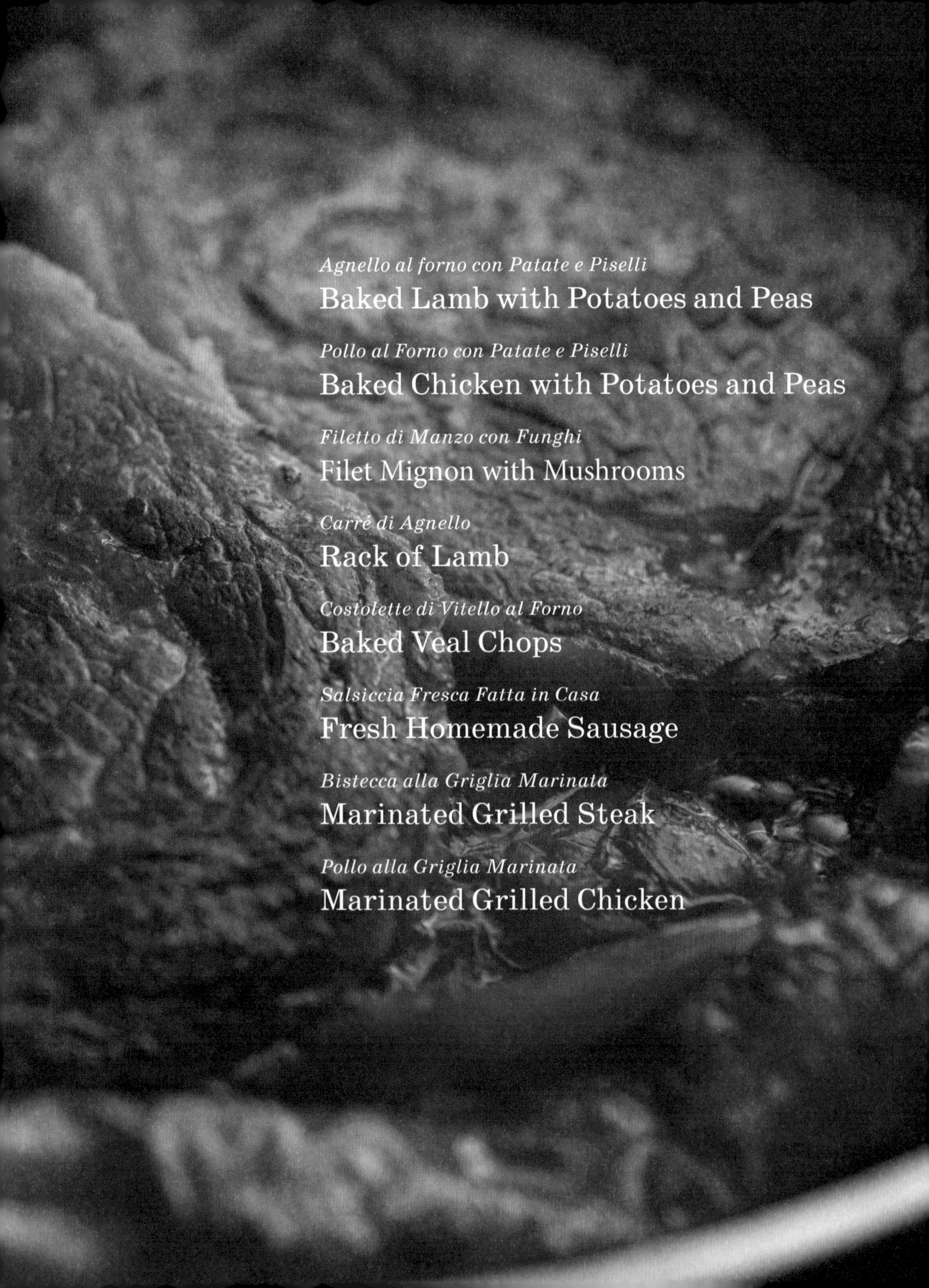

Agnello al forno con Patate e Piselli

Baked Lamb with Potatoes and Peas

Pollo al Forno con Patate e Piselli

Baked Chicken with Potatoes and Peas

Filetto di Manzo con Funghi

Filet Mignon with Mushrooms

Carré di Agnello

Rack of Lamb

Costolette di Vitello al Forno

Baked Veal Chops

Salsiccia Fresca Fatta in Casa

Fresh Homemade Sausage

Bistecca alla Griglia Marinata

Marinated Grilled Steak

Pollo alla Griglia Marinata

Marinated Grilled Chicken

Meats were eaten as a secondo piatto after pasta, soup, or legumes every night of the week except Wednesday and Friday, which were fish nights. Along with the meat, a salad and a contorno (or side dish) of vegetables were served. Every Saturday morning, my mother went shopping for the week's supply of meat at Phil the Butcher on 54th Street and New Utrecht Avenue in Brooklyn. When Phil retired, she went to Geraldo the Butcher a few blocks down. She purchased fresh steaks for Saturday night, since steaks were the one cut of meat that was never frozen. Her shopping list also included the meats for the Pork Sauce with Meatballs for Sunday dinner, stew meat, a chicken, and cutlets to freeze and then defrost during the week. She never froze meat for more than one week.

Makes about 13 medium meatballs or 9 dozen mini meatballs

1 pound ground meat (beef, pork, veal, or a combination)

2 large eggs

½ cup breadcrumbs

½ cup freshly grated cheese (Parmigiano Reggiano, Grana Padano, or Pecorino Romano)

¼ cup fresh parsley, finely chopped, optional

2 garlic cloves, minced, optional

⅛ teaspoon freshly ground black pepper

Extra virgin olive oil, for dipping

2 cups pure olive oil, for frying

Polpette
Meatballs

In our house, Sunday would not be a Sunday without meatballs. My mother usually made two types- fried and simmered in sauce. We always added the uncooked meatballs directly into the cooking sauce. She always made meatballs in batches of 13 in honor of the Feast of St. Anthony.

In a large bowl, add the ground meat, eggs, breadcrumbs, parsley and garlic (if using), grated cheese, and pepper. Thoroughly mix all the ingredients with your hands.

When all the ingredients are well combined, begin forming the meatballs. First, place a small amount of oil in a small bowl. Dip your fingers in the oil, and then spread the oil in the palm of your other hand. Take a piece of the meat mixture and roll it in the palm of your hands until it is uniformly round. The medium meatballs should each be about the size of a golf ball. The mini meatballs should each be about the size of a shelled hazelnut.

When all the meatballs are formed, they can be added directly to your sauce or fried according to the instructions below.

To fry meatballs:

In a 10-inch frying pan, add oil (about ½-inch in depth) and heat for 3 to 4 minutes on medium-high heat. To test the oil, place a pinch of the meatball mixture in the oil; if it begins to sizzle, the oil is ready. Add the meatballs in batches and continue to fry on medium heat until brown on all sides. Remove from the pan and place on a paper-towel lined dish to absorb excess oil.

Serve warm or at room temperature.

Serves 4 to 6

2 pounds cutlets, thinly sliced (chicken, veal, or pork)

1 cup whole milk

4 large eggs

3 tablespoons freshly grated cheese (Parmigiano Reggiano, Grana Padano, or Pecorino Romano)

2 tablespoons fresh parsley, finely chopped

1/8 teaspoon freshly ground black pepper

1½ cups breadcrumbs

4 cups pure olive oil, for frying

Cotolette "Impanate" (Pollo, Vitello o Maiale)

Fried Cutlets (Chicken, Veal, or Pork)

The secret to tender cutlets is marinating them in milk for a few hours before frying. I always fry extra cutlets and get two dinners out of the batch. The first night we would eat them fried and the second night I used them to make Cutlets Parmigiana.

Soak the cutlets in about one cup of whole milk for at least 4-12 hours, making sure they are completely covered by the milk. If making a combination of cutlets, soak the different meats separately.

Beat the eggs, grated cheese, parsley, and black pepper. Remove the cutlets from the milk, dip them in the egg mixture, and coat them in the breadcrumbs. Place on a dish and set aside.

In a 13" frying pan, add 4 cups of olive oil (about ½ inch in depth) and heat for a few minutes on medium high heat. To test the oil, place a pinch of the cutlet coating in the oil, if the oil begins to sizzle, the oil is ready. Add the cutlets in a single layer and lower heat slightly. Fry until golden brown on both sides. Remove from the pan and place on a paper towel lined dish to absorb excess oil.

Serve warm or at room temperature.

Note: As mentioned above, cutlets can be fried one day prior to use if making parmigiana style.

Serves 4 to 6

Fried Cutlets (see page 175)

1 26-ounce bottle passata di pomodoro

1 pound mozzarella cheese, shredded

Cotolette alla Parmigiana
(Pollo, Vitello o Maiale)
Cutlets Parmigiana (Chicken, Veal, or Pork)

Remember those extra fried cutlets? I use them to make one of my family's favorite dishes. There is no need to even cook the sauce. Just use good quality passata di pomodoro and shredded mozzarella.

Preheat the oven to 375°F.

In a baking dish large enough to fit all cutlets in a single layer, place a thin layer of passata di pomodoro. Then place the cutlets and cover each individual cutlet with a thin layer of additional passata and mozzarella. If the cutlets do not fit in 1 layer, either use another baking tray or place an additional layer of cutlets on top of the passata and mozzarella.

Cover the baking dish with aluminum foil and bake for 30 to 35 minutes or until the mozzarella is completely melted.

Let sit for about 15 minutes before serving.

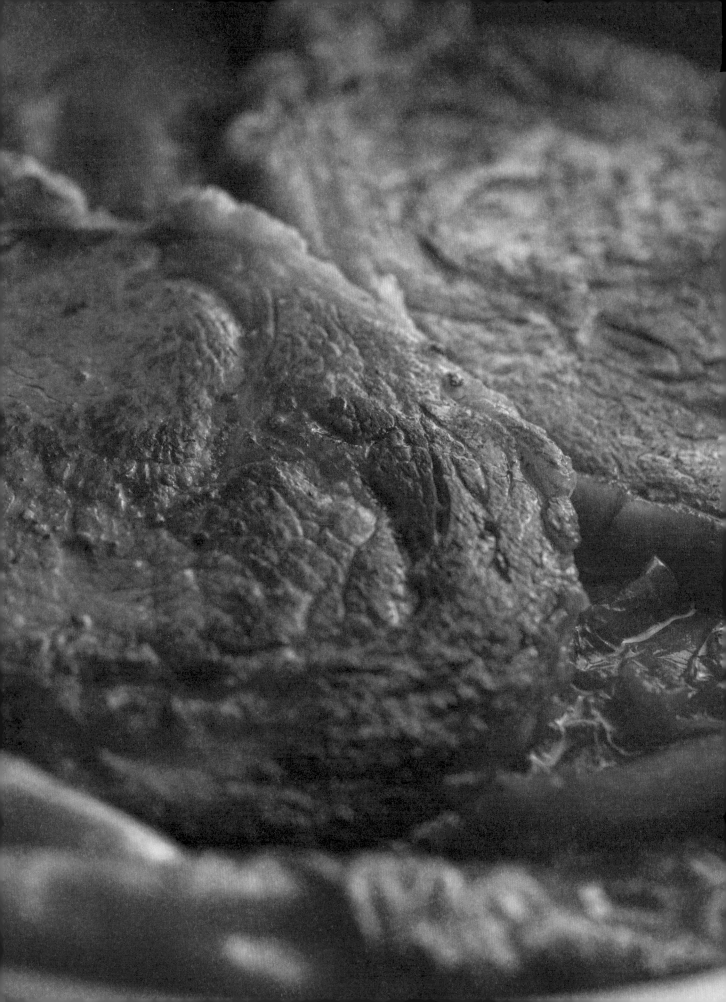

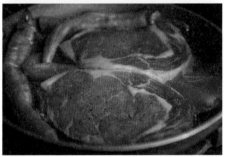

Serves 2

3 tablespoons pure olive oil

2 long hot green peppers

2 plum tomatoes, cut into quarters, cored, and seeded

2 boneless Rib Eye Steaks (about ¾ pound each)

Sea salt

Black pepper

Bistecca Rib-Eye con Peperoni e Pomodori

Rib-Eye Steak with Peppers and Tomatoes

This recipe is great during the winter when you are not able to barbecue outside. My father did not cook often but he loved to make this dish.

Season steaks all over with salt and pepper.

In a medium-size nonstick frying pan, add oil, peppers, and tomatoes. Heat for about 3 minutes on medium-low. Place a splatter cover on top of the pan to prevent any splattering oil.

Add the steak, increase the heat to medium, and cook on one side. Flip the steak over once and then cook on the other side until desired doneness is reached. (For medium-rare, cook to a temperature of 130°F.)

Top with the tomatoes, place the peppers on the side, and serve immediately.

Serves 4

2 pounds flank steak, sliced

2 teaspoons sea salt, plus more for seasoning

Freshly ground black pepper, for seasoning

7 tablespoons pure olive oil

1 large onion, sliced

1 garlic clove

½ pound white mushrooms, sliced

3 cubanelle peppers, cut into quarters, cored, and seeded

1 cup passata di pomodoro

Bistecca affettata con Funghi, Peperoni e Pomodori

Pepper Steak with Mushrooms, Peppers, and Tomatoes

This is a great dinner for anyone who likes lean meat. It is also a great party dish—it can be made in the morning and then reheated without losing any flavor.

Season steak with salt and pepper.

In a medium-size nonstick pan, place 3 tablespoons oil and heat for about 1 minute on high heat. Add steak and continue cooking on high heat for about 4 minutes. Rotate the pieces, making sure they brown on all sides. The meat does not need to be completely cooked.

Remove the meat from the pan, place in a dish, and discard excess liquid. Dry the pan with a paper towel.

Place 4 tablespoons oil, onion, and garlic in the pan. Heat on high for about 2 minutes.

Add the mushrooms, peppers, and 2 teaspoons salt and cook completely covered on medium heat for about 7 minutes, stirring occasionally.

Add the passata di pomodoro and mix all the ingredients well. Add the steak and continue cooking on medium heat, uncovered for about 5 minutes.

Serve warm.

Serves 4 to 5

2 pounds veal, cubed

5 links fresh sausage (about 1 pound)

½ cup extra virgin olive oil

¼ cup fresh parsley, chopped

1 large onion, sliced

5 fresh basil leaves, chopped

1 small fresh red hot pepper, optional

2 garlic cloves

1 large carrot, peeled and chopped into slices

1 celery stalk, chopped

1 teaspoon sea salt

Spezzatino di Vitello con Salsiccia

Veal Stew with Sausage

We make veal stew in the winter months because it is a hearty meal. This dish works great served over a bed of white rice or a dish of pappardelle. Make sure you have a loaf of bread on hand—you won't be able to stop dipping it in the stew!

In a large pot, place 4 cups of cold water, veal, and sausage and begin cooking on medium-high heat. When the water begins to boil, remove the veal and sausage and place in a colander. Cut each sausage into 3 pieces. Set aside.

In a nonstick sauté pan with a cover, place the oil, parsley, onion, basil, hot pepper (if using), and garlic and sauté on medium heat for 2 to 3 minutes, stirring occasionally.

Add the veal, sausage, carrot, celery, salt, and pepper and continue cooking on medium heat for about 10 minutes, stirring occasionally.

Add half the mashed tomatoes to the pan with ½ cup of boiling water. Return to a boil and continue cooking semi-covered for about 1 hour, stirring occasionally to make sure nothing sticks to the bottom of the pan.

Add remaining mashed tomatoes and an additional ½ cup of boiling water and continue cooking semi-covered for 45 minutes to 1 hour or until the veal pierces easily with a fork.

Let sit for 30 minutes before serving. If desired, serve over a bed of white rice or a plate of pappardelle.

Serves 4

1 rabbit, cut into 6 to 8 pieces (about 3½ pounds)

3 garlic cloves

1 small hot red pepper or 1 tablespoon pepper paste

1 large onion, sliced

½ cup fresh parsley, chopped

½ cup extra virgin olive oil

Sea salt, for seasoning

Black pepper, for seasoning

1 cup white wine

1 14-ounce can cherry tomatoes

10 ounces fresh cherry tomatoes, sliced in half

1 cup Gaeta or Taggiasca olives

Coniglio alla Cacciatora

Rabbit Cacciatore Style

Cacciatore-style or "hunter's style" is one of the most popular ways that Italians cook wild game and poultry. While most commonly served with chicken, rabbit produces a leaner and tastier dish.

Place the rabbit in a pot with 8 cups of cold water and begin cooking on medium-high heat. As soon as the water begins to boil, immediately remove the rabbit and place it in a colander. Set aside.

In a sauté pan with a cover, sauté the garlic, hot pepper, onion, ¼ cup parsley, and oil on high heat for 2 to 3 minutes.

Season the rabbit with salt and pepper. Add the rabbit to the pan and continue sautéing for about 3 minutes, mixing all the ingredients well.

Add the white wine and continue cooking on medium-high heat for another 6 minutes.

Add the remaining parsley, fresh and canned cherry tomatoes, olives, and ½ cup of boiling water and continue cooking uncovered for 5 to 7 minutes.

Reduce heat to medium-low and continue cooking completely covered for about 2 hours or until the meat easily falls off the bone. Stir occasionally.

Let sit for about 30 minutes before serving.

Note: Cooking time will vary depending on tenderness and size of the rabbit pieces. Add an additional ladle of boiling water if needed.

Serves 8 to 10

5 pounds tripe, cut into small pieces

1 lemon, cut into quarters

3 medium Yukon potatoes, cut into eighths

3 teaspoons sea salt, plus more for seasoning

2 large onions, sliced

½ cup extra virgin olive oil

3 garlic cloves

2 small hot or sweet red peppers

6 fresh basil leaves, chopped

¼ teaspoon freshly ground black pepper

2 28-ounce cans Italian whole peeled tomatoes

1 large carrot, peeled and sliced

2 cups frozen peas, rinsed in cold water

Trippa con Pomodoro, Patate e Piselli

Tripe with Tomato, Potatoes, and Peas

I vividly remember my mother scrubbing the tripe with oranges and lemon. She would use the citrus halves as if they were Brillo pads. Thankfully, this is not necessary. Today the tripe purchased in butcher shops is clean and just needs to be rinsed in water.

Rinse the tripe in cold water a few times.

In a large pot filled with cold water, place the tripe and lemons, making sure the water completely covers the tripe. Cook on high heat until it begins to boil. Then reduce heat to medium and continue cooking for approximately 1 hour. Remove the tripe with a slotted spoon, place in a colander, and set aside. Discard the lemon and water.

In a large bowl, add the potatoes and 1 teaspoon salt and completely cover with warm water. Set aside.

In a 6-quart sauté pot, sauté the onions, oil, garlic, peppers, and basil for 4 to 5 minutes.

Add the tripe, 2 teaspoons salt, and pepper to taste and mix well. Add a cup of boiling water and continue to cook on medium heat for about 30 minutes, stirring occasionally.

Using a vegetable mill, purée the canned tomatoes. Increase the heat to high and add the tomato purée. When the sauce begins to boil, reduce the heat to medium-low and continue cooking for about 15 minutes.

Remove the potatoes from the bowl of water and pat dry with a paper towel. Add the potatoes, carrots, and peas to the pot with the tripe and cook for about 1 hour on medium-low heat, stirring occasionally. If the sauce becomes too thick and the potatoes are still not cooked, add 1 to 2 ladles of boiling water. Additional salt can be added to taste, if needed.

Let sit for at least 30 minutes covered before serving.

Note: This dish can be made a few hours in advance and heated before serving. The tripe can also be cooked (with the lemon slices) 1 day in advance.

Serves 6 to 8

7 pounds baby lamb, cut into 3.5-inch pieces

2 cups red wine

3 tablespoons sea salt, plus more for seasoning

4 medium Yukon potatoes, washed, peeled, and cut into quarters

Freshly ground black pepper, for seasoning

2 small hot red peppers

2 large onions, sliced

6 garlic cloves

1 cup fresh parsley, chopped

4 plum tomatoes, seeded, cored, and cut into quarters

9 tablespoons extra virgin olive oil

1 28-ounce can Italian whole peeled tomatoes, mashed with a fork

2 cups frozen peas, rinsed in cold water and drained in colander

Agnello al Forno con Patate e Piselli

Baked Lamb with Potatoes and Peas

We always made baby lamb during the Easter season. My mother would place the lamb in a brine of salt, water, and wine. This would make the lamb sordirsci, which in the Calabrese dialect means "deafens" the lamb or removes its gamey taste.

Wash lamb in cold water and remove and discard excess fat.

In a large pot, create a brine of wine, 4 cups of cold water, and 2 tablespoons salt. Place the lamb in the brine and let sit for about 45 minutes.

Place the potatoes in a bowl with warm water and 1 teaspoon salt. Set aside.

Preheat the oven to 450°F.

Remove lamb from brine, place in a pot with 4 cups of cold water, and begin cooking on medium-high heat. When the water begins to boil, use tongs to remove the lamb and place in a colander. Set aside.

In a large baking dish (14.5-by-17.5-by-3 inches), place the lamb in a single layer and season with salt and pepper on all sides. Add the hot peppers, onions, garlic, parsley, plum tomatoes, ½ cup oil, half the mashed tomatoes, and 1 teaspoon salt. Cover the tray with aluminum foil and bake for 60 minutes.

Place the peas, remaining mashed tomatoes, 1 teaspoon salt, and 1 tablespoon oil in a bowl. Set aside.

Remove the baking dish from the oven, discard the foil, and reduce the oven temperature to 400°F. Use tongs to turn the pieces of lamb over.

Remove potatoes from bowl and pat dry. In a baking dish, sandwich the potatoes between two layers of lamb pieces. Top with the peas and remaining mashed tomatoes.

Continue cooking at 400°F uncovered for about 2 hours. About every 30 minutes, remove the baking dish from the oven, use tongs to turn the lamb, and pour the juices over the potatoes. The total baking time is about 3 hours or until the meat is tender and begins to pull away from the bone

Remove from oven, cover completely, and let sit for 20 minutes before serving. In a large serving platter, place the lamb pieces and potatoes and top with the peas and juice from the pan.

Serves 4

2 medium Yukon potatoes, washed,
peeled, and cut into quarters

1 whole chicken, cut into 10 pieces

2 large onions, sliced

2 large carrots, washed, peeled, and
cut into eighths

2 celery stalks, washed and cut into
quarters

2 garlic cloves

3 plum tomatoes, seeded, cored,
and cut into quarters

½ cup fresh parsley, chopped

Pure olive oil

Sea salt to taste

Black pepper to taste

1 cups frozen peas, rinsed in cold
water and drained in a colander

1 cup canned cherry tomatoes with
juice

Pollo al Forno con Patate e Piselli

Baked Chicken with Potatoes and Peas

A great dish served in the winter over a bed of white rice. This is another example of the double-boil cooking method, a technique that my mother used in many of her dishes. Since the chicken is being partially boiled before baking, the harsh fats are removed. The remaining chicken fat will keep it moist and flavorful. I recently purchased corned beef to prepare for Saint Patrick's Day and I asked the butcher for his cooking suggestion. His answer was "Cathy, do you know what double boil means?" I laughed and said "Yes, I know what to do."

Preheat the oven to 450°F.

Place potatoes in a bowl with warm water and ½ tablespoon salt. Set aside.

Rinse chicken and then place in a pot with 4 cups of cold water. Begin cooking on medium-high heat. Once the water begins to boil, remove chicken immediately and place in a colander. Discard water.

Remove potatoes from the bowl and pat dry. In a baking dish large enough to fit all the ingredients in a single layer, place chicken, onion, carrots, celery, garlic, plum tomatoes, and potatoes. Season with salt, pepper, parsley, and oil. Cover the baking pan tightly with aluminum foil and place in the oven for 60 minutes.

In a separate bowl, mix peas, canned tomatoes, ½ teaspoon salt, and ½ teaspoon oil. Set aside.

Remove the dish from the oven, discard foil, and reduce temperature to 400°F. Spread peas and canned tomatoes over chicken and mix well. Place the dish back into the oven and continue to cook for an additional 60 minutes or until chicken is tender and falling off the bone. Rotate the pan in the oven occasionally.

Place the pan under the broiler for about 3 minutes in order to brown the chicken.

Let sit for about 10 minutes before serving. Place on a serving platter and spoon the pan juices over the chicken and potatoes.

Serves 6 to 8

1 prime filet mignon, trimmed and tied (about 4 to 5 pounds)

Sea salt, for seasoning

Freshly ground black pepper, for seasoning

¼ cup aged balsamic vinegar

½ cup pure olive oil

2 large onions, sliced

8 ounces white button mushrooms, sliced

2 portobello mushrooms, sliced

Filetto di Manzo con Funghi

Filet Mignon with Mushrooms

Filet Mignon is always made on Christmas Day, Easter Sunday (in addition to the Baked Lamb with Potatoes and Peas), and Thanksgiving (in addition to a turkey). I always line the bottom of the baking pan with onions and mushrooms (white and portobello) and serve them as a side dish.

To make the marinade, place the filet mignon in a disposable pan and season on all sides with salt and pepper. Completely cover the filet with the vinegar and oil, add half the sliced onion, and mix well. Cover the pan and refrigerate overnight.

Remove the pan from the refrigerator about 1 hour before roasting.

Preheat the oven to 500°F.

In a roasting pan with a rack, add the mushrooms and remaining onion under the rack. (For additional flavor, also add the sliced onions that marinated with the filet.) Season the mushrooms and onions with salt and pepper. Place the rack over the mushrooms and onions and then place the filet on top.

Place the roasting pan in the oven and bake for 15 minutes. Flip the filets and continue cooking for another 5 minutes.

Reduce heat to 400°F, flip the filets again, and continue cooking for 30 to 35 minutes or until desired temperature is reached (130°F for medium-rare). Once desired temperature is reached, remove from the oven.

Let sit for 10 minutes before serving.

Serves 4 to 6

2 racks of lamb, frenched (about 1¾ pounds each)

Sea salt, for seasoning

Freshly ground black pepper, for seasoning

1 bunch fresh parsley, finely chopped

2 garlic cloves

2 tablespoons red wine vinegar

¾ cup olive oil

Carré di Agnello

Rack of Lamb

This is a very easy dish to make and very impressive to serve. Each rack of lamb is enough for two to three people. This is best served medium-rare.

Season rack of lamb with salt and pepper.

In a baking dish (9-by-13-by-2 inches), marinate the lamb with parsley, garlic, vinegar, and oil. Refrigerate overnight.

Remove from the refrigerator 1 hour before baking.

Preheat the oven to 475°F.

Transfer the lamb to a large, rimmed baking sheet or pan with a rack. Place the lamb upright, crossing the bones of both racks.

Bake the lamb for 15 minutes. Rotate the pan and reduce the heat to 400°F. Continue to cook for about 15 more minutes or until a thermometer inserted in the center reads 130 to 134°F (for medium-rare) or 135 to 144°F (for medium).

Let sit for 10 minutes before serving.

Serves 4

4 veal chops (about ¾ pound each)
2 cups whole milk
¾ cup breadcrumbs
4 tablespoons pure olive oil
1 small onion, finely sliced
1 14-ounce can Italian whole peeled tomatoes
½ teaspoon sea salt

Costolette di Vitello al Forno
Baked Veal Chops

This was another of our winter dinners when it was too cold to grill. The secret to this dish is to soak the veal chops in milk before cooking. You'll also place the veal chops under the broiler for a few minutes after baking to ensure that the breadcrumbs are crispy.

In a large, wide, covered container, place the veal chops in milk, making sure the milk covers the veal chops. Let them soak in the refrigerator for 2 to 3 hours.

Preheat the oven to 375°F.

Remove the veal chops from the milk. Using your hands, evenly coat both sides of veal chops in breadcrumbs. Set aside.

In a baking dish (9-by-13-by-2 inches), place the oil, onion, tomatoes, and salt. Mash the tomatoes with a fork, mix all ingredients, and evenly spread throughout the dish. Place the dish in the oven for 5 minutes.

Remove the dish from the oven and place the veal chops in the dish in a single layer. Bake for 20 minutes.

Remove the dish from the oven and use tongs to flip the veal chops. Return dish to the oven and continue to bake for another 20 minutes or until an internal temperature of 160°F (for medium) is reached. Cooking time will vary depending on the thickness of veal chop.

Change the oven setting to broil and place the dish under the broiler for about 2 minutes.

Let sit for a few minutes before serving. Top with tomato, onion, and juices from the baking dish.

10 pounds pork butt, coarsely ground (a ratio of about 80% meat to 20% fat)

½ cup fine sea salt

¼ cup hot pepper powder or paprika

¼ cup crushed red chili pepper flakes

1 tablespoon whole black pepper, crushed with a mortar and pestle

½ cup red wine

1 cup sweet or hot pepper paste

32 to 35 mm natural hog casings (enough for 20 to 25 pounds of meat)

1 lemon, cut in quarters

Butcher's twine

Sausage pricker or large sewing needle

Salsiccia Fresca Fatta in Casa
Fresh Homemade Sausage

There is nothing like the taste of homemade sausage. This is the only recipe in the book that I learned from my father.

When I was young, I always made sausage with my parents in the back of the store during the winter months. First, we would clean the bone-in pork butts. Since my father insisted that some of the meat be cut by hand, we would make two batches, one hand-cut and the other machine-ground. When fresh sausage is cured, it becomes dry sausage or soppressatta depending on the casing used. My mother-in-law would hang the fresh sausage in a cold room for a few days and then slice it into thick pieces that she'd fry in oil. Somewhere between fresh and cured, the taste was quite unique.

This recipe is very simple and doesn't require any expensive equipment; all you need is a sausage-stuffing machine. Ask your local butcher to grind the pork butt. Buy double the sausage casing, as half of the casings always tear during the stuffing process.

Homemade sausage is great on the grill or in Sunday Sauce with Meatballs and Sausage. It can be frozen for up to two months.

Spread the pork meat in a large metal or plastic tray. The pile should be approximately 3-inches high.

Evenly spread the salt, pepper powder, crushed red and black pepper, wine, and pepper paste onto the meat. Mix well.

In a cold room, let the mixture sit for approximately 2 hours.

To clean the casings, rinse them under cool running water, removing the salt they are packed in. Then fill the casings with cold water, discard the water, and repeat the process. Fill a bowl with cold water and place the casings and lemon in the bowl. Let soak for at least 2 hours. Keep them soaking right until the time of use. They must be moist when placed on the stuffing tube, otherwise they will be difficult to fill.

Put the casing on the stuffer tube and tie the end with the twine. Begin filling the casings as tight as possible. As you go along, lightly prick the sausage with a sewing needle or sausage pricker, removing any air pockets. Tie each link and continue stuffing, or, stuff the complete casing and tie the links when done. If the casing tears, do not try to repair it. Just tie the casing and continue. It is best to stuff when the casings are moist. If they become dry while on the funnel, take a handful of water and moisten the casings.

The sausage can be used immediately or stored in the refrigerator (for up to 2 days) or freezer.

Note: If you wish to make sweet sausage, use sweet pepper powder and sweet pepper paste. Eliminate the crushed red pepper and double the black pepper amount.

Marinates about 3 steaks

⅓ cup pure olive oil

¼ cup fresh parsley, chopped

3 tablespoons red wine vinegar

2 garlic cloves, cut in halves

3 rib-eye steaks

Sea salt, for seasoning

Bistecca alla Griglia Marinata

Marinated Grilled Steak

This marinade works great on any steak or short ribs. During the summer months, we would barbecue every Saturday. My fondest memories of Saturday night barbecues were at our first home on 59th Street in Brooklyn. We did not have a backyard, just a rooftop patio. I remember starting the charcoal on the barbecue with wood sticks. As soon as the flame began, I would fan the grill with newspapers so the fire would spread.

In a bowl, combine the oil, parsley, vinegar, and garlic. Season the steaks with salt and then place in a baking dish with the marinade. Let sit in the refrigerator for at least 1 to 2 hours.

Remove the baking dish from the refrigerator about 1 hour before beginning to grill.

Preheat the grill.

Grill the steaks for about 3 to 4 minutes on each side, until 130°F for medium-rare.

Serve immediately.

Pollo alla Griglia Marinata

Marinated Grilled Chicken

Saturday nights were always barbecue nights. In addition to our family favorites of steak and sausage, we always had chicken.

Serves 4

1 cup orange juice, fresh squeezed

2 tablespoons extra virgin olive oil

2 garlic cloves, sliced

½ cup fresh parsley, chopped

½ teaspoon dry Italian oregano

1 whole chicken, cut into 10 pieces (about 3.5 pounds)

Sea salt, for seasoning

Freshly ground black pepper, for seasoning

In a bowl, mix orange juice, oil, garlic, parsley, and oregano. Set aside.

Wash chicken and remove and discard excess fat. Pat dry with a paper towel. Season chicken with salt and pepper.

Place the chicken in a disposable pan with the marinade and mix well. Cover the pan with aluminum foil and let marinate in the refrigerator for 2 to 4 hours.

Preheat the barbecue to about 500°F.

Place the disposable pan with the marinated chicken on the grill for about 10 minutes.

Remove the chicken from the pan and place directly on the grill. Discard the pan and marinade. Barbecue the chicken until well-cooked or an internal temperature of 165°F is reached. Remove from the grill and cover with aluminum foil.

Let sit for 10 minutes before serving.

Vegetables

Patate Bollite
Boiled Potatoes

Patate al Forno "Panate"
Mashed Baked Potatoes

Fagiolini con Aglio e Aceto
String Beans with Garlic and Vinegar

Fagiolini con Patate "Panate"
String Beans with Mashed Potatoes

Erbe Bollite con Patate
Dandelion Greens with Potatoes

Bietole con Patate e Cannellini
Swiss Chard with Potatoes and Cannellini Beans

Asparagi Bolliti
Boiled Asparagus

Friarielli Bollite
Boiled Broccoli Rabe

Melanzane alla Parmigiana
Eggplant Parmigiana

Melanzane Soffritti
Sautéed Eggplant

Polpette di Melanzane Fritte
Fried Eggplant "Meatballs"

Fava e Piselli con Pancetta
Fava and Peas with Pancetta

Peperoni Lunghi Piccante Arrostiti
Roasted Long Hot Peppers

Asparagi al Forno
Baked Asparagus

Soffritto di Peperoni, Cipolle e Pomodori
Sautéed Peppers, Onions, and Tomatoes

Zucchine al Forno con Cipolla
Baked Zucchini with Onion

Insalata di Cicoria e Scarola
Chicory and Escarole Salad

Insalata di Pomodoro e Patate
Tomato and Potato Salad

As vegetables are the focal point of the Calabrese diet, this chapter is the largest in the book. In my family, we always ate "verdure scadata," Calabrese for boiled vegetables (in Italy, they are called "verdure bollite"). My mother boiled the vegetables and then placed them on a serving platter. At the table, we each added our preferred quantities of extra virgin olive oil—we never added oil over whole dish. There were often leftovers, but we never refrigerated oiled vegetables in the same container as those without. We poured fresh oil on top of the leftovers only after taking the vegetables out of the fridge.

It is absolutely essential to prepare vegetables that are ripe and in season. When I was growing up, my father had a vegetable garden on the roof of our Brooklyn house. He cut used olive barrels in half and filled them with soil to use as planters. Once vegetables ripened, we cooked them almost immediately to capture their goodness. As we had a bumper crop of each vegetable, we devised many ways to cook each one.

Our salads were composed of chicory, escarole, romaine, iceberg lettuce, fennel, or a combination of these greens. To dress the salad, we tossed the lettuce with red wine vinegar (never balsamic), extra virgin olive oil, and salt. There was no such thing as a salad dressing.

Yukon, red, or russet potatoes

Patate Bollite
Boiled Potatoes

We always boil potatoes whole and with their skin for extra flavor. I always make a few extra and cut them up the next day. They are delicious when you fry them with a few tablespoons of olive oil and serve as a side dish. You can also fry them with eggs to make an even better breakfast.

Scrub and wash potatoes, making sure not to remove skin. Place them in a large pot and fill with cold water until covered by about 2 inches.

Bring to a boil and then reduce heat to medium. Continue cooking uncovered for 25 to 35 minutes or until a fork easily pierces through the potatoes. Cooking time will vary based on the size of the potatoes. Remove immediately.

If mashing, peel potatoes and discard the skin. Mash immediately in a vegetable mill, potato ricer, or with a fork.

If using in a recipe that calls for sliced or cubed potatoes, let cool at least 1 to 2 hours before cutting. The potatoes can be refrigerated overnight before cutting. Peel potatoes and cut according to recipe specification.

Note: Potatoes should all be the same size so that the cooking time will be the same for each potato.

Serves 4 to 6

4 large russet potatoes

2 tablespoons extra virgin olive oil, plus more for serving

½ teaspoon sea salt

Patate al Forno "Panate"

Mashed Baked Potato

Mashed baked potatoes were always made to accompany any assortment of grilled meats. Unlike most Americans, my family never wrapped the potatoes in aluminum foil before placing in the oven. Additionally, butter was never used to season—only olive oil and sea salt.

Preheat the oven to 400°F.

Wash and scrub potatoes. Pat dry with a paper towel.

Place the potatoes directly on the lower rack of the oven and let bake for about 45 minutes or until a knife pierces through the skin easily. Remove from the oven.

Immediately remove the outer skin and mash with a fork in a serving bowl. Add oil and salt, adjusting for taste.

Serve warm with additional oil to taste.

2 pounds Italian flat string beans

2 teaspoons sea salt

*6 tablespoons white wine vinegar
(minimum 6% acidity)*

5 tablespoons extra virgin olive oil

2 garlic cloves, finely chopped

Fagiolini con Aglio e Aceto

String Beans with Garlic and Vinegar

This recipe is great for summer barbecues. The beans can be made early in the day and seasoned about an hour before serving.

Remove top and bottom stems of string beans and discard. Rinse well in cold water.

Bring 8 cups of cold water to a boil. Add string beans and salt and return to a boil and continue cooking for about 20 minutes or until the beans are tender. Drain well and let cool.

Once cooled, add vinegar, oil, and garlic and mix well.

Serve at room temperature.

1 ½ pounds Italian flat string beans

2 medium Yukon potatoes, washed and scrubbed

3 teaspoons sea salt, plus more for seasoning

Extra virgin olive oil, for seasoning

Fagiolini con Patate "Panate"

String Beans with Mashed Potatoes

This recipe is one of the many ways to prepare string beans, which grow in abundance during the summer months. The potato starch given off during the cooking gives the string beans an added flavor.

Remove top and bottom stems of string beans and discard. Rinse well in cold water.

In a large pot with 3 quarts of cold water, add potatoes and salt and bring to a boil. Continue to cook for about 15 minutes.

Add string beans and continue cooking until the potatoes are easily pierced with a fork and the string beans are tender, about 30 minutes.

Remove the potatoes from the pot and place in a large bowl. Peel and discard the skin. Mash the potatoes with a fork.

Using a slotted spoon, remove string beans and add them to the bowl with the potatoes. Mix the potatoes and string beans. Add oil and additional salt to taste. If a bit dry, add some of the cooking liquid.

Serve warm.

Serves 4

1 bunch dandelions (about 1½ pounds)

2 large or 3 medium Yukon potatoes, scrubbed and washed

¾ tablespoon sea salt, plus more for serving

½ cup extra virgin olive oil, plus more for serving

2 garlic cloves

Dandelion Greens with Potatoes

Also known as "wild greens," dandelion is a vegetable that has many health benefits. This is one dish that I enjoy eating in Italy since each region's "wild green" is unique. The hardest part of making this recipe is washing the dandelion, since it grows low to the ground and the leaves are very dirty. Sauté the garlic with the reserved cooking liquid and olive oil.

Cut about 1 inch of the bottom stem of the dandelion and discard. Wash each leaf individually and then cut into 2-inch pieces. Wash well again and set aside.

In a pot with 12 cups of cold water, place potatoes and bring to a boil. Continue to cook on medium heat for about 10 minutes.

Add dandelions and salt, using a spatula to press down on the dandelions, and continue cooking on medium heat for about 13 minutes. Use a slotted spoon to remove dandelions, place in a colander, and set aside. Once the potatoes pierce easily with a fork, remove from the pot. Reserve ½ cup of cooking liquid.

Peel the potatoes and discard the skin. In a large bowl, mash the potatoes with a fork.

Heat the reserved cooking liquid, oil, and garlic for about 2 minutes. Add dandelions and mashed potatoes and continue cooking on medium-low heat for about 3 minutes, continuously mixing. Discard garlic.

Serve warm. If desired, top with additional salt and oil to taste.

Serves 4

1 bunch Swiss chard (about 1½ pounds)

1½ teaspoons sea salt, plus more for serving

⅓ cup extra virgin olive oil, plus more for serving

1 garlic clove

1 14-ounce can Italian cannellini beans, rinsed and drained

1 medium Yukon potato, boiled, peeled, cooled, and cut in large cubes (see page 208)

Bietole con Patate e Cannellini

Swiss Chard with Potatoes and Cannellini Beans

Swiss chard is another vegetable with many health benefits and is less bitter than some of the other leafy greens. Swiss chard is great just boiled and topped with olive oil, but this combination is very unique and simple to make.

Remove and discard about 1 inch of Swiss chard stem. Wash each leaf individually and then chop into 1½-inch pieces. Wash another 2 to 3 times. (Swiss chard is a very sandy vegetable).

Bring 6 cups of water to a boil in a large pot, add Swiss chard and salt. Cook semi-covered on medium heat, for about 10 minutes, occasionally pressing down on the vegetables.

Drain in colander, reserving ⅓ cup of the cooking liquid.

In a medium sauté pan, add oil, garlic, reserved liquid, cannellini beans, and potatoes. Cook on medium heat for about 3 minutes. Add Swiss chard, mix well, and continue cooking for another 3 to 5 minutes.

Serve warm. If desired, top with additional oil and salt to taste.

Asparagi Bolliti
Boiled Asparagus

Asparagus is loaded with nutrients and antioxidants. Always cook asparagus in a wide pot so the stalks can be placed horizontally. This is typically served as a side dish.

Serves 6

2 bunches asparagus (about 2½ pounds)

2 teaspoons sea salt

Extra virgin olive oil, for serving

Trim and discard the bottoms of each asparagus spear (about 1 inch). Rinse the asparagus a few times in cold water and place in a colander.

In a wide stock pot, bring 6 cups of water to a boil and add asparagus and salt. Continue to cook uncovered on medium heat for about 8 minutes or until desired tenderness is reached.

Serve warm or at room temperature. Top with oil to taste.

Note: Cooking time will vary depending on the thickness of asparagus.

Friarielli Bollite
Boiled Broccoli Rabe

This is my favorite of all vegetables. Broccoli rabe is known for its slightly bitter taste. I often make an extra bunch or two and leave them in the refrigerator. We usually use the leftovers as a side dish or on a sandwich throughout the week.

Serves 4 to 6

2 bunches broccoli rabe (about 2½ pounds)
1 tablespoon sea salt
Extra virgin olive oil, for serving

Trim and discard about 1-inch of the broccoli rabe stems. Then, peel each stem and discard any random leaves. Wash well, keeping the broccoli rabe in the same direction.

Bring 8 cups of water to a boil and add broccoli rabe and salt, keeping all the stems in the same direction. Occasionally, use a spoon to press the broccoli rabe down below the water's surface. Cook semi-covered on medium heat for 6 minutes.

Carefully remove the broccoli rabe with a fork and place on a serving platter.

Serve warm or at room temperature. Top with oil to taste.

Serves 5

1 large eggplant or 2 medium eggplant (about 2 pounds)

1 tablespoon sea salt

2 large eggs

2 cups breadcrumbs

3 cups pure olive oil, for frying

½ pound mozzarella cheese, shredded

1 26-ounce bottle passata di pomodoro

Melanzane alla Parmigiana

Eggplant Parmigiana

This recipe is unique because the eggplant is cut into thick, round slices. The eggplant can be fried in advance and then baked about 30 minutes before serving.

Wash eggplant and remove and discard the stem. Slice eggplant into ½-inch or ¾-inch round slices. Sprinkle the slices with salt, place in a colander, and cover with a plate. Add a weight (such as a can of tomatoes) to press down and help drain the eggplant. Let sit for 30 minutes to 1 hour.

Rinse off the salt with cold water, squeeze out the excess water, and pat dry with a paper towel.

In a small bowl, beat the eggs. Dip the eggplant slices in the egg and then the breadcrumbs. Continue until both sides of each slice are covered in both. Place on a dish and set aside.

In a 12-inch pan on medium high heat, add oil (about ½-inch in depth). To test the oil, place a pinch of the eggplant mixture in the oil; if it begins to sizzle, the oil is ready. Without crowding, add the eggplant in batches in a single layer and then reduce heat slightly. Fry until golden brown on each side. Place on a paper towel-lined dish to absorb excess oil.

Preheat the oven to 375°F.

In a wide baking dish, spread a thin layer of passata di pomodoro, then add all of the eggplant slices (if possible), and top with mozzarella and remaining passata. If the eggplant cannot fit in one layer, repeat for a second layer. This dish is best if prepared in a single layer.

Bake covered for about 30 minutes or until all the mozzarella is melted.

Serve warm.

Serves 6

4 small eggplants

4¼ teaspoon sea salt

1 large Yukon potato, peeled and cut in eighths

½ cup extra virgin olive oil

1 large onion, sliced

2 garlic cloves

10 fresh basil leaves, finely chopped

2 cubanelle peppers, seeded, cored, and cut into quarters

1 14-ounce can Italian cherry tomatoes

Freshly grated cheese (Parmigiano Reggiano, Grana Padano, or Pecorino Romano), for serving

Melanzane Soffritti

Sautéed Eggplant

This is another dish that requires a few loaves of bread for dipping. We always made this in the summer months, as a side dish to grilled meats or as a secondo piatto. If we had leftovers, my mother would make lunch the next day by poaching or scrambling a few eggs in the eggplant ratatouille.

Wash eggplant, remove and discard stems, and cut into quarters. Sprinkle the pieces with 1 tablespoon salt, place in a colander, and cover with a plate. Add a weight (such as a can of tomatoes) to press down and help drain the eggplant. Let sit for 1 hour.

Place the potatoes and ¼ teaspoon salt in a bowl filled with warm water, enough to cover the potatoes. Set aside.

Rinse eggplants, remove excess salt, and then squeeze them to remove excess water. Pat dry with a paper towel.

In a large nonstick sauté pan with a lid, heat the oil, onion, and garlic for 1 minute on medium heat. Then add the eggplant and basil and mix well. Cover the pan and continue to cook for 5 minutes, stirring occasionally. Add the potatoes, peppers, 1 teaspoon salt, and cherry tomatoes. Mix well and make sure the potatoes are on the bottom layer of the pan.

Continue cooking completely covered on low heat for an additional 40 minutes. If needed, add a ladle or two of boiling water. Stir occasionally and make sure the ingredients are not sticking to the bottom.

Let sit for at least 15 minutes before serving. If desired, top with freshly grated cheese.

Makes about 9 "meatballs"

1 large eggplant or 2 medium eggplant (about 2 pounds)

1 tablespoon sea salt

1 large egg

12 fresh basil leaves, finely chopped

2 garlic cloves, minced

¾ cup breadcrumbs

1 cup freshly grated cheese (Parmigiano Reggiano, Grana Padano, or Pecorino Romano)

2 cups pure olive oil, for frying

Polpette di Melanzane Fritte

Fried Eggplant "Meatballs"

If you enjoy meatballs, you must try this meatless recipe. Even some of my carnivore friends enjoy this more than my regular meatballs. The eggplant can be boiled the night before and then refrigerated in a colander to drain overnight.

Wash eggplant, remove and discard stem, and cut into eighths. Place eggplant and salt in a pot with enough cold water to cover eggplant by an inch. Bring to a boil and continue cooking for 15 minutes. Immediately drain in a colander and let cool.

Gently remove and discard the eggplant skin and then finely chop the eggplant. In a large bowl, mix the chopped eggplant, egg, basil, garlic, breadcrumbs, and grated cheese. Continue mixing with your hands until all the ingredients are evenly distributed.

Take a small amount of the mixture and roll into a ball the size of a golf ball. Continue until all the eggplant meatballs are formed.

In a 10-inch frying pan, add oil (about ½-inch in depth) and heat for 3 to 4 minutes on medium heat. To test the oil, place a pinch of the eggplant mixture in the oil; if it begins to sizzle, the oil is ready. Add the eggplant meatballs in a single layer. Reduce the heat slightly and fry until golden brown in color on all sides. Place on a paper towel-lined dish to absorb excess oil.

Serve warm.

Note: Because the water content of eggplant can vary, add additional breadcrumbs if the mix is not binding.

Fava e Piselli con Pancetta

Fava and Peas
with Pancetta

This is one of my signature Calabrese dishes. Frozen fava beans are readily available throughout the year in most specialty stores.

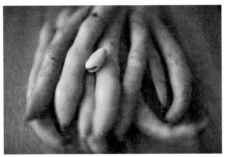

Serves 6

6 ounces pancetta (preferably Flat Pancetta Calabrese-Style, see page 248)

1 28-ounce bag frozen fava beans or 5 pounds shelled fresh fava beans

14 ounces frozen peas

1 medium onion, sliced

2 teaspoons sea salt

Extra virgin olive oil, for seasoning

Remove the outer skin of the pancetta and discard. Cut the pancetta into cubes and place in a bowl with 2 cups of hot water for about 3 to 4 minutes. Discard water and set pancetta aside.

Rinse the fava beans and peas in cold water. Place in a colander and set aside.

In a large pot, place 5 cups of cold water, pancetta, and onion and bring to a boil.

Add fava, peas, and salt to the pot and continue cooking semi-covered on high heat until the water begins to boil. Reduce heat to medium-low and continue cooking semi-covered for 25 to 30 minutes. (Cooking time will vary depending on the tenderness of the fava and peas.)

Let sit for about 10 minutes before serving. Top with oil to taste.

Peperoni Lunghi Piccante Arrostiti
Roasted Long Hot Peppers

This is a simple dish that goes well with grilled meats, as an appetizer, or on sandwiches.

Serves 6 to 8

12 long hot green peppers
4 long hot red peppers, optional
Sea salt, for seasoning
Extra virgin olive oil, for seasoning

Preheat the oven to 375°F.

Rinse the peppers in cold water and pat dry with a paper towel.

Place the peppers in a single layer on a parchment-lined baking sheet and place in the oven. Bake for 15 minutes and then use tongs to flip each pepper. Continue baking for an additional 15 to 20 minutes or until the peppers are blistering.

Remove from the oven and let cool. Skin does not need to be removed. Season with salt and oil to taste.

Serves 4 to 6

1 bunch asparagus (about 1 pound)

1 teaspoon sea salt

2 large eggs

_4 tablespoons freshly grated cheese
(Parmigiano Reggiano or Grana
Padano)_

1½ cups breadcrumbs

_2 tablespoons pure olive oil, plus
more for greasing_

Asparagi al Forno
Baked Asparagus

_This can be a very simple side dish or appetizer. It can be prepared
in advance and served at room temperature._

Preheat the oven to 375°F.

Wash the asparagus in cold water and remove and discard about 1 inch
of each spear.

In a pot that is wide enough to fit the asparagus horizontally, place 3
cups of cold water and the asparagus, keeping them all in the same
direction. Bring to a boil. Continue to cook on medium-high heat for
about 2 minutes. Remove and place asparagus in a colander.

Beat the eggs and grated cheese.

Individually dip each asparagus spear in the egg mixture and then in
breadcrumbs. Place on a dish and set aside.

Lightly grease a baking dish (9-by-13-by-2 inches) with oil. Place the asparagus in a single layer on the baking dish and drizzle 2 tablespoons oil
on top. Place in the oven and bake for about 25 minutes. Occasionally
remove the tray from the oven and gently move the asparagus with a fork
to make sure they are not sticking to the bottom of the pan.

Remove the tray from the oven. Switch oven to broil and place tray under the broiler for 1 to 2 minutes.

Let cool before serving.

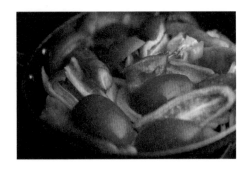

Sautéed Peppers, Onions, and Tomatoes

As a kid, I never put ketchup on my hamburger or mustard on my hot dogs. Instead, I would top them with sautéed peppers, onions, and tomatoes.

Serves 6

1 large onion, sliced

3 cubanelle peppers, seeded, cored, and cut into quarters

3 tomatoes, seeded, cored, and cut into quarters

½ teaspoon sea salt

1 garlic clove

⅓ cup extra virgin olive oil

In a medium nonstick sauté pan, place onion, peppers, tomatoes, salt, garlic, and oil. Mix well and begin cooking on high heat.

When it begins to sizzle, reduce heat to medium-low, mix ingredients, and continue cooking completely covered for 25 to 30 minutes. Stir occasionally.

Serve warm.

Zucchini al Forno con Cipolla

Baked Zucchini with Onion

This is a great dish for the summer, when zucchini is in abundance.

It works great as a side dish to any protein.

Serves 6

6 small zucchini (2½ to 3 pounds)

1 large onion, sliced

6 fresh basil leaves, chopped

2 garlic cloves

½ teaspoon sea salt

½ cup extra virgin olive oil

1/8 teaspoon freshly ground black pepper

⅓ cup freshly grated cheese (Parmigiano Reggiano, Grana Padano, or Pecorino Romano)

Preheat the oven to 375°F.

Wash zucchini, remove and discard stem, and cut into eighths.

In a baking dish (9-by-13-by-2 inches), place zucchini, onion, basil, garlic, salt, oil, and pepper. Mix all the ingredients well. Cover the tray with aluminum foil and place in the oven for about 40 minutes.

Remove the baking dish from the oven. Reduce the heat to 350°F, discard foil, and mix all the ingredients. Return to oven for another 30 minutes or until the zucchini is soft. Top with grated cheese.

Let sit for 10 to 15 minutes before serving.

Insalata di Cicoria e Scarola

Chicory and Escarole Salad

This recipe is a unique combination of bitter greens. It was made whenever we made Escarole, Chicory, and Fennel Soup. The outer leaves were used for the soup and the tender inner leaves were used for the salad.

Serves 2 to 4

1 head escarole, inner leaves

1 head chicory, inner leaves

Italian red wine vinegar (minimum 6% acidity), for dressing

Extra virgin olive oil, for dressing

Sea salt, for dressing

Wash the individual leaves of the chicory and escarole. Cut them into 1-inch pieces and wash again. Let drain in the colander for about 1 hour.

Place the chicory and escarole leaves in a salad bowl. Drizzle with vinegar, oil, and salt to taste.

Insalata di Pomodoro e Patate

Tomato and Potato Salad

The secret to this recipe is using high-quality olive oil and sweet ripe tomatoes during the summer months.

Serves 6 to 8

2 large Yukon potatoes, boiled (see page 208)

1 beefsteak tomato or 3 plum tomatoes, sliced

1 fresh pepper (red hot, jalapeno, or cubanelle), sliced

6 fresh basil leaves, chopped

2 garlic cloves, cut in halves

¾ teaspoon sea salt, plus more for serving

½ teaspoon dry Italian oregano

¼ red onion, sliced

⅓ cup extra virgin olive oil, plus more for serving

Prepare Boiled Potatoes according to recipe.

Once cooled, peel the potatoes, cut into quarters, and then cut again into thick slices. In a large bowl, add the potatoes, tomatoes, pepper, basil, garlic, salt, oregano, and onion and mix well.

When ready to serve, add the oil and mix well again. If desired, top with additional salt and oil to taste.

Jarred, Cured, and Pickled Foods

Pomodori Conservati
Home-Jarred Tomatoes

Lupini Ammollati
Soaked Lupini Beans

Olive Verdi Fresche Schiacciate
Fresh Cracked Green Olives

Melanzane Sott'aceto
Pickled Eggplant

Peperoni Arrostiti
Roasted Peppers

Pomodori Secchi Sott'olio
Sun-Dried Tomatoes in Oil

Pancetta Piatta alla Calabrese
Flat Pancetta Calabrese-Style

Food preservation was an integral part of Calabrese cuisine. The main reason for preserving was to prevent waste. It also supplied families with foods throughout the year that were only available seasonally. Vegetables that could not be eaten within a short time were jarred. They then lasted for a full year and were primarily served as antipasti. Traditionally, they were stored in "cuniettos"—round clay pots. Similarly, a pig was slaughtered only once a year, during the week leading up to Carnivale or Fat Tuesday. It was almost impossible to consume the entire animal in the week or two that the meat would remain fresh, but curing it allowed the pork meat to be enjoyed for many months.

While food in Italy was preserved for very practical reasons, my family continued to cure meats and pickle vegetables in Brooklyn. That's because the taste of our home-preserved food was incomparable. My children loved visiting my father-in-law's house when he cured meats. He would show them his shed where dozens of sausages and soppressata were hung to cure.

Both in Calabria and in Brooklyn, only salt and vinegar were used for preservation. Nitrates were never added. Regardless of what was being preserved, we made sure to remove the air and moisture in order to keep the preserved food for up to a year.

When I was a schoolgirl, my mother often packed pickled eggplant or peppers stuffed with anchovies in my lunch box. Most of my friends stared in awe as they watched me eat. They were unwrapping peanut butter and jelly sandwiches and had never before seen an anchovy-stuffed pepper. While many people remember going to the beach with their friends for Labor Day, my memory is of canning tomatoes with my family on the last days of summer.

Pomodori Conservati

Home-Jarred Tomatoes

This recipe produces two 1-quart jars of tomatoes. To yield only 1 quart, just use about 2¾ pounds of tomatoes. My mother would always pick Labor Day weekend for this. It took two days, as we jarred at least ten bushels of tomatoes. We never puréed the tomatoes. We cut them in half and packed the jars and added a basil leaf and salt to each. At times, my mom would add a small hot pepper to some of the jars.

Tomatoes were not the only thing jarred that weekend. We would also blanch red roasting peppers and make the pepper paste needed to make the different salamis in the winter.

Makes 2 1-quart jars

5½ pounds ripe plum tomatoes

3 teaspoons sea salt

4 basil leaves

4 small fresh hot pepper, optional

2 1-quart, wide-mouth Ball canning jars, sterilized

Wash tomatoes, remove and discard the stem, and cut the tomato in half. Remove and discard inner stem and seeds. Place in a colander and set aside.

Evenly distribute salt, basil, and pepper between each jar. Add tomatoes and press firmly with a wooden spoon into the jar as you go. Use your hands to firmly pack the tomatoes at the end.

Fill the jar completely until ½ inch from the rim. Cover with the lid and close tightly with the metal band.

Place the jars in a large pot with cold water, making sure the water completely covers the jars by a few inches. Bring to a boil, reduce heat, and continue cooking for approximately 30 minutes. Remove the jars once water is cool.

The following day, make sure each jar has sealed. If it has not sealed, the jar must be kept refrigerated and used within a few days. If it has sealed, store in a cool, dark place for up to 1 year.

Makes 3 1-quart jars

2 pounds dry lupini beans

3 1-quart Ball canning jars, sterilized

3 tablespoons sea salt, plus more for serving

Lupini Ammollati

Soaked Lupini Beans

Lupini beans are a very healthy snack because of their high protein and fiber content. We make them during the Christmas season and eat them throughout the year.

Rinse the lupini beans in cold water and discard any branches or pebbles.

In a pot with cold water, place the beans and bring to a boil. Remove the beans immediately and discard the water.

Place the beans in a plastic container or large pot with cold water, making sure the water completely covers the beans. Replace with fresh cold water twice a day for 6 days.

In each canning jar, place 1 tablespoon salt. Use a slotted spoon to divide the beans and fresh cold water between all 3 jars, leaving about 1 inch of space below the rim. Cover with the lid and close tightly with the metal band.

Place jars in a large pot filled with cold water, making sure the water covers a few inches above the jars. Bring to a boil, reduce heat, and continue boiling for approximately 30 minutes. Let the jars sit in the water until the water is cool and then remove the jars.

The following day, make sure each jar has sealed. If it has not sealed, the jar must be kept refrigerated and used within a few days. If it has sealed, store the jar in a cool, dark place for up to 1 year. Keep refrigerated after opening.

If desired, add salt to taste before serving.

Note: Alternatively, the lupini beans do not need to be jarred. If desired, conclude the recipe before boiling jars in water and place directly in the refrigerator, keeping for up to 2 weeks.

Olive Verdi Fresche Schiacciate
Fresh Cracked Green Olives

This is another one of my mother-in-law's recipes. She would make these olives every year around mid-September or early October. The olives can be purchased at your local fruit store or online at Penna Olives.

Makes 2 quarts

8 pounds fresh Colossal Green Olives

12½ tablespoons coarse sea salt, plus more for seasoning

1 lemon, cut in quarters

2 garlic cloves, sliced

1 hot red pepper, sliced

2 stalks celery, thinly sliced

½ cup extra virgin olive oil

½ teaspoon dry Italian oregano, for seasoning

Remove olive stems and leaves and then rinse olives. Wearing plastic gloves so that your hands do not stain, remove the pits. You can either do this with an olive pitter or hit once with the flat side of a meat tenderizer and then remove the pit.

Bring 4 quarts of water to a boil. Add olives and continue cooking for 30 seconds, continuously stirring. Immediately drain in a colander and set aside.

In a large plastic bucket or ceramic container, add the olives, 4 quarts of fresh cold water, 2½ tablespoons salt, and lemon. Let sit for 24 hours. Once a day, replace the water and salt but keep the same lemon. Continue this process for 5 days and then drain in a colander and discard the lemon.

Place olives in a plastic container or glass jar and season with garlic, hot pepper, celery, oil, salt, and oregano to taste. Keep refrigerated for up to 1 month.

Makes 2 16-ounce jars

5 large eggplant (about 6 pounds)

1 cup coarse sea salt

18 garlic cloves, peeled

4 cups celery, chopped

¼ cup small dry hot peppers, or less to taste

1 17-ounce bottle Italian white wine vinegar (6% acidity minimum)

Pure olive oil, for jarring and serving

2 16-ounce wide-mouth Ball canning jars, sterilized

Melanzane Sott'aceto

Pickled Eggplant

We would make pickled eggplant once a year in September, storing the eggplant in a cunieto, the Calabrese name for a clay pot used for pickling. The clay pot had a round wooden disk on top. A boulder was then placed on top of the disk to press down on the eggplant. The resulting taste was amazing! The recipe below produces the same flavor but uses a more modern technique. I use a vegetable squeeze and canning jars. For best results, wait a few weeks before eating the eggplant after canning.

Wash eggplant and remove and discard stems. Peel the eggplant, discard the skin, and then slice vertically. Stack the slices and then cut into ½-inch strips.

Place the eggplant in a round plastic tub and mix well with salt. Place a dish with a weight on top of the eggplant, pressing down, and let sit for about 6 hours.

Without rinsing the eggplant, squeeze and discard excess salt and water. Rinse the plastic tub and then add the eggplant, garlic, celery, and peppers. Mix well and add the vinegar. Cover again with a weighted dish for about 12 hours.

Transfer to a vegetable squeeze for about 24 hours. (Alternatively, you can place in a colander and cover again with a weighted plate for 24 hours.)

Remove all ingredients from the vegetable squeeze. In small batches, begin filling the canning jars, pressing down with a wooden spoon as you go and adding more of the eggplant mix. Fill until about 1 inch from the rim. Then, fill the jar with as much oil as it takes to fill up any excess space, still leaving the top 1 inch of the jar empty. Cover with the lid and close tightly with the metal band.

Place the jars in a large pot filled with cold water, making sure the water covers a few inches above the jars. Bring to a boil, reduce heat, and continue boiling for about 30 minutes. Let the jars sit in the water until the water is cool and then remove them from the water.

The following day, make sure each jar has sealed. If it has not sealed, the jar must be kept refrigerated and used within a few days. If it has sealed, store the jar in a cool, dark place for up to 1 year.

When serving, top with additional oil to taste. Once the jar is open, keep refrigerated and use within 2 weeks.

Makes 3 16-ounce jars

10 red and yellow bell peppers (5 to 6 pounds)

3 16-ounce wide-mouth Ball canning jars, sterilized

3 teaspoons sea salt, plus more for serving

Extra virgin olive oil, for serving

Dry Italian oregano, for serving

Peperoni Arrostiti
Roasted Peppers

While there is nothing like a fresh roasted pepper, the longevity from the canning process allows these to be enjoyed any time of year. This is the perfect addition to any grilled meat or sandwich.

Preheat the oven to 450°F.

Wash the peppers, dry with a paper towel, and place on a parchment-lined baking sheet.

Reduce the oven temperature to 400°F and place the baking sheet in the oven. Bake for about 20 minutes. Flip the peppers over and continue baking for about another 20 minutes. The outer skin should be blistering.

Remove from oven and immediately place the peppers in a closed Ziploc bag or brown paper bag. Let sit for about 5 minutes.

Remove peppers from the bag and then remove and discard outer skin, stems, and seeds. Set aside.

Place 1 teaspoon salt in each canning jar. Add the peppers and press down firmly with a wooden spoon. Fill the jar until about 1 inch from the rim. Cover with the lid and close tightly with the metal band.

Place the jars in a large pot with cold water, making sure the water completely covers a few inches above the jars. Bring to a boil, reduce heat, and continue boiling for about 30 minutes. Let the jars sit in the water until the water is cool and then remove the jars from the water.

The following day make sure each lid has sealed. If it has not sealed, the jar must be kept refrigerated and used within a few days. If it has sealed, store the jar in a cool, dark place for up to 1 year.

When serving, top with oil, oregano, and additional salt to taste.

Note: Alternatively, the peppers do not need to be jarred. If desired, conclude the recipe before placing the peppers in jars and serve immediately or keep refrigerated for up to 2 days.

Makes 2 16-ounce jars

2 cups Italian white wine vinegar (minimum acidity 6%)

17 ounces sun-dried Italian tomatoes

2 16-ounce wide-mouth Ball canning jars, sterilized

4 tablespoons salted nonpareil capers

2 tablespoons dry Italian oregano

Pure olive oil, for jarring

Pomodori Secchi Sott'olio

Sun-Dried Tomatoes in Oil

My father was one of the first importers of sun-dried tomatoes in America. I remember seeing them for the first time and wondering: What could you possibly do with them? Many years later, they have become a staple in the Italian-American pantry.

In a large pot, add the vinegar and 2 cups of water and bring to a boil. Add the dry tomatoes, making sure the tomatoes are completely submerged, and continue boiling for about 3 minutes.

Drain the tomatoes in a colander and let sit for about 30 minutes.

Spread the tomatoes evenly on 2 paper towel-lined baking sheets. Let them air dry for 24 hours, turning the tomatoes twice a day.

Rinse the capers and dry them with a paper towel.

In each canning jar, add a few tomatoes, sprinkle some oregano and capers, and press down with a wooden spoon. Repeat this process, creating layers, until about 1 inch from the rim. Then, fill the jar with as much oil as it takes to fill up any excess space, still leaving the top 1 inch of the jar empty. Cover with the lid and close tightly the metal band.

Place the jars in a large pot filled with cold water, making sure the water a few inches above the jars. Bring to a boil, reduce heat, and continue boiling for about 30 minutes. Let the jars sit in the water until the water is cool and then remove from the water.

The following day, make sure each jar has sealed. If it has not sealed, the jar must be kept refrigerated and used within a few days. If it has sealed, store the sealed jar in a cool, dark place for up to 1 year.

Once the jar is opened, keep refrigerated and use within a few weeks.

Note: Alternatively, if using within 1 month, conclude the recipe after filling the jars with the ingredients and oil. Place in the refrigerator. About 1 hour before serving, remove the jar from the refrigerator and leave at room temperature.

1 piece pork belly with skin (about 7 pounds)

1½ cups coarse sea salt

1 cup red wine

1/3 cup hot or sweet pepper paste

1½ tablespoons hot or sweet pepper powder

10 tablespoons crushed red chili pepper flakes

Butcher's twine

Flat Pancetta Calabrese-Style

As a young girl, my family would make pancetta in the winter months. We would buy pork belly, remove the bones, and save them for Sunday's Pork Sauce with Meatballs and Sausage. Twice a day, for two days, we would massage the pork belly with brine and sea salt. Then we would wash off the salt with red wine and top the pancetta with pepper paste, pepper powder, and crushed red pepper. Then we hung it in a cold place for five to seven weeks. Pancetta is great sliced thin or used in many dishes. My favorite is Fava and Peas with Pancetta. If you prefer, you can use sweet pepper paste and sweet pepper powder so the pancetta is milder.

Place pork belly in a large, flat plastic tub and completely cover both sides with salt.

Massage the salt into the pork belly, making sure you get it in any creases or openings. Repeat every 12 hours, for a total period of 48 hours. As the salt begins to cure the pancetta, liquid will seep from the meat to create a salt brine. Use this liquid together with the salt to keep massaging. Every time the meat is massaged, flip it over so that it rotates between the skin side up and the skin side down. Store the pancetta in the refrigerator during this process.

After the 2-day brining period, discard brine and excess salt. Rinse the plastic tub and then return the pancetta to the tub.

In the tub, rinse off the excess salt on the pancetta with the red wine. Pat dry.

Place pancetta on a flat surface, skin-side down. Wearing disposable gloves, rub the pepper paste evenly along the pancetta. Then sprinkle the pepper powder and the crushed red pepper. Gently pat the pepper into the pancetta.

About 2 inches from the top, use a paring knife to make a small incision and place a piece of butcher's twine through it. Tie a knot at the end of the twine, creating a hook to hang the pancetta. Make sure the twine is thick enough to hold the pancetta.

Hang the pancetta in a cool, dry basement room for 5 to 7 weeks. The room temperature should be 50 to 60°F.

Once it is fully cured, the pancetta can be stored in the refrigerator for 4 to 5 weeks or longer if vacuum-sealed.

Note: This should only be made in the winter months of December, January, or February. Above measurements are a guideline and will vary according to the size of the pork belly.

Breads
and Sweets

Pane Fatto in Casa
Homemade Bread

Friselle
Double-Baked Bread

Pane Pasquale ("Gutá")
Easter Bread

Pizza Chiena
Pizza Rustica

Fichi al Forno
Baked Figs

Biscotti di Fichi di Natale ("Pité")
Christmas Fig Cookies

Zeppole con Acciughe ("I Zippuli")
Zeppole with Anchovies

My mother made bread in the winter while my mother-in-law baked it throughout the year. If my mother-in-law had any leftover bread, she ground it into breadcrumbs which gave her fried food an amazing color and taste. Today, I store old bread in a brown paper bag. Once the bag is full and the bread is dried, I use a box grater to create my own breadcrumbs. If you don't want to make them yourself, I recommend purchasing breadcrumbs from a local bakery rather than the commercial kind that's sold in round boxes in the supermarket. Trust me, you'll notice the difference!

Desserts were rarely served in the homes of either my mother or my mother-in-law. Dinner always ended with fruit and coffee. When we had guests, they brought bakery pastries like cannolis, sfogliatelle, and napoleons. While neither of them baked cakes, both of these matriarchs made Calabrese holiday specialties: Easter Bread, Christmas Fig Cookies, and Zeppole with Anchovies. We served panettone during Christmas and the dove-shaped cake called Colomba di Pasqua after Easter dinner. There were always Italian cookies on hand to serve with coffee or tea or as an afternoon treat.

Makes 20 to 24 medium-small rolls

5 pounds unbleached all-purpose flour (about 17 cups), plus more for baking sheet

3 ¼-ounce packets active dry yeast

2½ tablespoons sea salt

Pane Fatto in Casa

Homemade Bread

My mother was devoted to Saint Anthony and would always make bread on his feast day that took place on June 13th. Every year, we would make small rolls in batches of thirteen and bring them to church to get blessed. My mother-in-law would add pieces of flat pancetta to the bread before placing it in the oven.

Sift flour onto a clean, flat surface. Make a well in the center.

In a bowl, add yeast and ¾ cup of warm water (100 to 110°F). Mix well until it begins to bubble. Let rest for 3 to 4 minutes.

Pour the yeast mixture into the center of the well and begin mixing with the flour. This will create a lumpy flour.

Gradually add 5 cups of warm water, continue mixing. Add salt.

Continuously knead and fold the dough for at least 20 minutes. Then, divide the dough into 5 pieces, rearrange the pieces, and knead them back into 1 piece of dough. Repeat this process 2 additional times to ensure perfect consistency.

Place dough in a large pot and cover with a lid and warm blanket . Place in a warm, dark place and let sit for about 1 hour and 30 minutes.

Begin kneading dough into any of the following desired shapes:

1. To create a bagel-like shape, use a scale to measure 5 ounces of dough. Gently roll dough into a log. Transform into a circular shape by bringing the two ends together and connect them by pinching tightly.

2. To create an oblong roll, use a scale to measure 9 ounces of dough. Gently roll dough into a log. While pinching the center of the log, bring the two ends together and align the dough in a parallel fashion.

3. To create a traditional roll, use a scale to measure 3 ounces of dough. Gently roll on a flat surface to create a ball shape and then pat slightly to flatten.

After forming each shape, use a knife to place 2 small slits on the dough.

Place the shaped dough directly on a bedsheet-lined table and cover with the blanket and an additional sheet. Let rise about 1 hour.

Preheat the oven to 425°F.

Lightly flour a baking sheet and place the shaped doughs onto the baking sheet, making sure they are not too close together.

Bake on the lower rack for about 12 minutes.

Move the tray to the upper rack for an additional 6 to 8 minutes or until the bread is golden in color. Remove from oven and cool on a rack.

Place a second tray on the lower rack and repeat the above process. A tray on the upper and lower rack may be placed in the oven at the same time.

Bread will stay fresh for a few days stored in a covered container or it can be frozen for a few weeks.

Friselle

Double-Baked Bread

Whenever we baked Homemade Bread, it would be impossible to eat all the bread within a few days. My mother would make half of the dough into different shapes. She then used the other half of the dough to make friselle, or double-baked bread.

Prepare Homemade Bread according to recipe.

As soon as the bread is removed from the oven, slice in half and place on a baking sheet with the slit side up. Set aside.

When all the bread is baked, reduce the oven to 250°F.

Return the baking sheets with the sliced bread to the oven for 30 minutes. Turn off the oven and leave the trays in until the oven is cold.

Remove and let completely cool. Store in a covered container for up to 2 weeks.

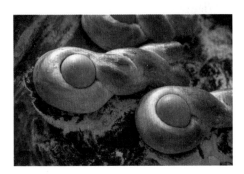

Makes 12 Easter Breads

Starter:

2 ¼-ounce packets active dry yeast
¾ cup unbleached all-purpose flour

Bread dough:

2 pounds 00 or all-purpose flour
(6½ cups), sifted, plus more for
baking sheet
1 cup sugar
17 large eggs
½ cup extra virgin olive oil
¾ cup warm milk

Pane Pasquale ("Gutá")
Easter Bread

Known to the Calabrese as gutá, this Easter Bread was always made on Holy Thursday. My sister-in-law's mother, Rosa Commisso, made the best Easter Bread. Each year she would come to my home on the night of Holy Thursday and bring us her gutá. In the old days, Easter Bread was eaten on Holy Saturday with the homemade soppressata and sausage that had been cured since Carnevale. This recipe calls for 2 pounds of flour which yields about a dozen Easter Breads. When I made this recipe with my mother, we would make at least sixty to give to family and friends.

For the starter:

In a bowl, mix 1 cup of warm water (100 to 110 °F) and yeast. Let sit for 3 to 4 minutes. Add the flour and mix well.

Place in a large pot with a lid. Cover the pot with a warm blanket and place in a warm spot overnight.

The next morning, the starter should have the consistency of cake batter.

For the bread dough:

In a large baking dish or clean flat surface, mix the flour and sugar and make a well. In the center of the well, add 4 eggs, oil, milk, and starter dough. Begin kneading.

Knead for about 20 minutes and then slice the dough into 3 pieces. Place these pieces on top of each other and knead back into 1 piece of dough. Repeat this process twice.

Place the dough in a large pot with a lid. Wrap a blanket around the pot and place in a warm place for about 2 hours and 30 minutes.

Place 12 whole eggs in a large pot with cold water. When the water begins to boil, reduce the heat to medium-low and continue to cook for 3 minutes. Remove the eggs and pat dry with a paper towel. Set aside.

After the dough has risen, you can begin to form the bread. Take a 5-ounce piece of dough and roll it into a log. Place 1 boiled egg in the center of the log and crisscross the remainder of the dough. Repeat this

process until 12 breads are formed or all the dough is used up.

Place the bread directly on a bedsheet-lined table and cover with a blanket. The loaves should be placed in an orderly manner, according to when they were formed so that you can bake the first one formed, followed by the second, and so forth.

Preheat the oven to 375°F.

Lightly flour a baking sheet. Transfer the first few breads to the baking sheet.

In a small bowl, beat the last egg until foamy. Lightly brush the dough with the egg wash.

Place on the lower rack of the oven and bake for 10 minutes, rotating the tray once halfway through baking.

Move the tray to the upper rack and continue cooking for another 10 minutes or until the breads are golden brown in color. When the first tray is moved to the upper rack, another tray may be placed on the lower rack.

Crust:

*2 pounds 00 or unbleached all-pur-
pose flour (6½ cups), sifted, plus
more for baking dish*

2 teaspoons baking powder

1¼ teaspoon sea salt

*1 cup unsalted butter, chilled and
cubed, plus more for baking dish*

5 large eggs

Filling:

3 large eggs

1 pound fresh ricotta, drained

*2 pounds assorted cured meats
(preferably soppressata or dry sausage, prosciutto, and mortadella),
cubed*

*2½ pounds assorted cheese (prefer-
ably primo sale, basket, and provolone cheese), cubed*

Pizza Chiena

Pizza Rustica

Pizza Rustica is a stuffed meat pie made by Southern Italians around Easter time. While my mother did not make this while I was growing up, my daughter and I decided to try and create this dish. The buttery, flaky crust combined with the cheesy and savory filling quickly became a favorite among our friends and family. Now we find ourselves making this dish every year to celebrate the holiday.

For the crust:

In a medium bowl, combine the flour, baking powder, and salt. Add in the butter and mix until flaky. Add 4 eggs and 1 cup cold water. By hand or using an electric stand mixer, knead until all ingredients are evenly distributed and a firm dough is formed.

Divide the dough into 2 pieces (portioned into 1/3 and 2/3 of the dough), wrap each piece in plastic wrap, and let sit at room temperature for about 20 minutes.

Preheat the oven to 375°F.

Butter and flour a deep, rectangular baking dish (14.5-by-11-by-3 inches). Roll out the larger portion of dough and transfer into the dish, pressing it smoothly against the bottom and sides of the pan. This dough should be big enough to cover the height of the pan. Let sit while you make the filling.

For the filling:

In a large bowl, beat 3 eggs until frothy. Then add the ricotta and mix until well combined.

Fold in the cubed cheeses and meats.

Pour evenly into the prepared baking dish.

Roll out the remaining piece of dough and cover the filling entirely. Using a fork, pinch the edges of the top and bottom layers of the dough together to form a seal. Using a knife, cut a few slits into the top dough.

In a small bowl, beat the last egg until foamy. Brush the entire top of the dough with the egg wash.

Bake the pie for about 1 hour and 15 minutes or until the crust is golden and the filling is puffed. Let cool before serving.

Serves 8 to 10

1 pound Italian dry figs, sliced in halves

½ pound almonds or walnuts, shelled

¼ teaspoon cinnamon

Zest of 1 orange

Anisette liqueur, for serving

Fichi al Forno

Baked Figs

This sweet treat was commonly made in December, since the dried figs were shipped from Italy in November. We always served them as one of our many desserts for Christmas Eve. If you store this dish in an airtight container, it can last for weeks.

Preheat the oven to 300°F.

Separate the sliced figs into 2 piles. Using 1 pile of figs, place 1 almond or walnut in each side of the fig.

Sprinkle the filled figs with cinnamon and orange zest.

Cover each filled fig with an unfilled fig. Press both halves firmly together.

Place the figs on a parchment-lined baking sheet. Bake for 15 minutes and then turn the figs over and rotate the pan. Continue baking for another 15 minutes or until the figs are golden brown in color.

Lightly drizzle Anisette liqueur over the figs.

Let cool completely before serving.

Makes 22

Fig filling:

17 ounces Italian dry figs

½ cup white raisins

1 cup walnuts, shelled and finely chopped

1 cup almonds, shelled and finely chopped

¾ cup brewed Italian espresso, sweetened with 1 teaspoon sugar

1½ cup vincotto

4 ounces dark chocolate, melted in a double boiler

2 teaspoons cinnamon

Zest of ½ orange

½ tablespoon cloves, finely crushed with a mortar and pestle

Biscotti dough:

2 pounds 00 or unbleached all-purpose flour (6½ cups), plus more for baking sheet

1 cup sugar

3 3-gram packets Paneangeli vanilla powder

¾ cup whole milk

5 teaspoons baking powder

6 large eggs

½ cup extra virgin olive oil

Biscotti di Fichi di Natale ("Pité")
Christmas Fig Cookies

We always make pité—the Calabrese name for fig cookies—the week before Christmas. These are one of my favorite cookies. My mother's secret for the biscotti dough was that the number of teaspoons of baking powder was equivalent to the number of eggs. She also used extra virgin olive oil instead of butter. The figs and nuts would be cut a few nights before the cookies were baked, then cooked and refrigerated. The reason for this was so the nuts and figs would absorb all the flavors. When I was young, vincotto was not readily available in America so we made our own during wine season. Now it is readily available in Italian specialty stores. I remember hearing stories from fellow Calabrese telling us the American version of vincotto was Bosco Chocolate Syrup!

For the fig filling:

Remove and discard the fig stems and rinse under cold running water. Pat dry and then finely chop into small pieces.

Rinse the raisins in cold water. Pat dry then chop.

In a large pot with a lid, combine the figs, raisins, walnuts, almonds, espresso, vincotto, chocolate, cinnamon, orange zest, and cloves. Mix well.

Place on the stove and cook on low heat continuously, mixing for 5 to 7 minutes. Cooking time will vary depending on the thickness of vincotto.

Remove covered pot from heat and let cool. Place in the refrigerator for 2 to 3 days. Once a day, remove from refrigerator and mix.

For the biscotti dough (to be prepared when ready to bake the cookies):

In a large baking dish or clean flat surface, sift the flour and then mix in the sugar and vanilla. Make a well in the center of the flour.

In a small sauce pan, warm the milk on low heat for about 3 minutes. Remove from heat and dissolve baking powder in the milk. It will begin foaming.

Pour the milk mixture, 5 eggs, and oil into the well.

Mix together and then begin kneading the dough. After about 5 minutes of kneading, slice the dough into 3 pieces. Place these pieces on top of each other and knead back into 1 piece of dough. Repeat this process twice.

Preheat the oven to 375°F.

Take 3 ounces of the dough and flatten into an oval shape. Cut 3 slits into the upper half of the oval-shaped dough.

Take 1 tablespoon of the fig mixture and place it in the center of the oval dough. Close tightly and press the edges with your fingers, removing any excess dough. It will resemble a small calzone. Knead the excess dough into the original dough. Continue this process until all the dough is used.

Lightly flour a baking sheet and place the first batch of cookies. In a small bowl, beat the last egg until foamy. Lightly brush each cookie with the egg wash.

Place on the lower rack of the oven for about 10 minutes and then move to the upper rack for another 10 to 15 minutes or until golden brown. When the first tray is moved to the upper oven rack, another tray may be placed on the lower rack. Let cool completely before serving.

Note: If you do not have espresso, increase the vincotto by ¾ cup.

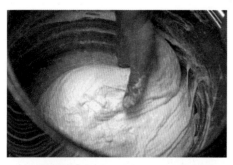

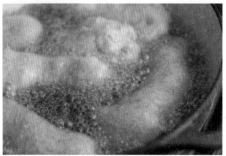

Makes 24 to 30

2 pounds russet potatoes, boiled
(see page 208)

2 tablespoons sea salt

2 pounds 00 flour (6½ cups)

1 ounce fresh yeast

2 3-ounce jars Italian anchovies in
olive oil (about 24 anchovies)

10 cups pure olive oil, for frying

(see page 208)

Zeppole con Acciughe ("I Zippuli")
Zeppole with Anchovies

The zippuli—the Calabrese word for zeppole—were always made on Christmas Eve, New Year's Eve, and Saint Joseph's Day, which also happened to be my father's birthday. On Christmas Eve and New Year's Eve, my mother would make the dough in the afternoon and begin frying right after dinner was finished. The zippuli were a symbol of celebration and happiness. It should be noted that this may be one of the most difficult recipes in the book. If you do not succeed on your first try, do not give up. There are three secrets to this recipe: use the same ratio of potatoes to flour, break the rise of the zeppole dough, and use russet potatoes.

Prepare Boiled Potatoes according to recipe.

Peel the potatoes and discard the skin. Using a potato ricer, mash the potatoes into a large, stainless steel baking dish or on a clean flat surface, creating a small mound about 3 to 4 inches high. Add 1 tablespoon salt and mix well.

Sift the flour over the potatoes. Sprinkle 1 tablespoon salt and gently mix the flour and salt into the potato mound with your hands. Create a well in the center of the mixture.

In a separate bowl, add the yeast and 1 cup of warm water (100 to 110°F) and mix well. Let sit for 3 to 4 minutes.

Pour the yeast mixture slowly into the center of the well and begin kneading all the ingredients.

In a clean bowl, add ¼ cup of warm water and set aside.

Using a dough scraper, scrape any excess flour back into the dough. Continue kneading and folding for 10 to 15 minutes. Dip fingers in the water bowl 1 to 2 times during this kneading process to create a sticky dough. Use additional water or flour as needed.

In a large pot with a lid, add 2 teaspoons of water and the kneaded dough. Cover the pot with a warm blanket and set in a warm, dark place. Let rise for about 2 hours. After rising, the dough should be about 2½ times its original size.

Refill the bowl of water with 1/4 cup fresh warm water. Dip your fingers in the bowl with warm water. To break the rise of the dough, make a fist and gently push down the center, deflating it, and then fold the edges into the center until the dough is about its original size. Let the dough rise again for another 1½ hours or until the dough is about 2½ times in size again.

When the dough is ready, remove the anchovies from the jar, discard the oil, and place on a paper towel-lined dish. Set aside.

In a small bowl, place ¾ cup of water. Set aside.

In a 6-quart pot, heat oil (about 2 inches in depth) to a temperature of 350°F. When the oil is ready, dip your fingers in the water, and grab a golf ball-sized piece of dough. Add an anchovy to the center, twist and pull, and immediately drop into the oil. Repeat process until the zeppole fit in the pan in a single layer, making sure not to overcrowd. Once the zeppole turn golden in color, flip them and continue frying until golden on all sides. (It is best to have two people during this step, one preparing the dough for the oil and the other frying the zeppole.)

Remove the zeppole and place on a paper towel-lined dish to absorb excess oil.

Serve warm or at room temperature.

Note: For a sweet variation, you can eliminate the anchovies from the center and top with powdered sugar.

Index of Recipes

Ricordo di Calabria

Acknowledgements

This book would not have been possible without Daniel Paterna, my photographer, book designer, and a true artist. He captured my love of food in the photographs that accompany these recipes. There are simply no words to express my gratitude to him for making my dream of writing a cookbook a reality.

I am grateful to my publisher, Daniel Power, for believing in both The Italian Daughter's Cookbook *and me. I want to extend my heartfelt gratitude to Naomi Falk, my exceptional Production Director whose immense talent was instrumental in bringing this book to life. A special thank you goes to my incredibly skilled editor Sophie Golub, for her invaluable contributions. Thank you to Daniel Spencer Esq, for his time and dedication. My friend Sharon Franke supported my dream of creating my mother's recipes. My love for Calabrese cooking and my family, as well as my beautiful memories, came alive on the page thanks to her editing. Many of the serving pieces in the photographs were generously provided by Angela Richards of Steelite International.*

I thank my nephew Salvatore Pugliese for being a very special person in my life. Throughout this entire project, my sister-in-law Rosa Fazzolari gave me her love and support. I am grateful to my neighbor Roberta Chavis, who has given me many years of friendship and love. A special thanks to Vincenzo Ruggiero, who always believed in this book. Anna Amendolara Nurse introduced me to the world of cookbooks, and I cherish the many books she has gifted me over the years.

Ingrid Diasparra, Liliana Bruschi, and Sandra Doria are treasured friends who helped me edit these pages.

I will forever be grateful to my mother-in-law for sharing her passion for cooking with me, Alessandra, Domenico, and Isabella.

My father always believed in me and gave me the courage to have dreams and the ability to realize them. My mother's stories and her recollections of my family history live in these pages and in my heart.

Lastly and most importantly, I want to thank my husband and children—my life, my purpose! I love them more than anything! Joe's unconditional love gave me the strength to achieve this very special goal. I am grateful for his assistance throughout this process.

*To Alessandra, Domenico, and Isabella who helped with everything from cooking to cleaning, writing to editing, testing to tasting, I say, "I love you more than you can ever imagine." I am truly blessed! And a very special thanks to Isabella, who has been helping me with this book since she was a little girl. She assisted me in recreating the recipes, measuring and recording the ingredients as I cooked, and then editing them once they were written down. Isabella is an amazing cook in her own right. I promised her that one day we would have all the family recipes in a book and here it is—*The Italian Daughter's Cookbook. *To our next book together!*

Cathy Coluccio Fazzolari is co-owner of the legendary D. Coluccio & Sons in Brooklyn, New York. Founded by her late father in the mid-1960s, D. Coluccio & Sons is one of the oldest importers of Italian specialty foods in the United States, with a retail store adjacent to the wholesale location. Cathy grew up in the business. She is fluent in Italian and has a bachelor's degree in marketing from St. John's University in Queens, New York. Today, she runs the day-to-day operations of the company, travels to Italy, and attends trade shows to source artisanal food products. She has a passion for food and learned to cook from her mother, who was a native of Calabria, Italy. Cathy has taught cooking classes at the Great Neck Adult Center, New York City College of Technology, and Boston College. Cathy has served on the board of Les Dames d'Escoffier New York as treasurer and is a member of the National Organization of Italian American Women (NOIAW).

The Italian Daughter's Cookbook
Authentic Calabrese Recipes

Photographs © 2024 Daniel Paterna
Text © 2024 Cathy Coluccio Fazzolari

Published in the United States by powerHouse Books,
a division of powerHouse Cultural Entertainment, Inc.
32 Adams Street, Brooklyn, NY 11201-1021

www.powerHouseBooks.com

First edition, 2024

Library of Congress Control Number: 2024936370

ISBN 9781648230660

Design by Daniel Paterna

Printed by SiZ Industria Grafica

10 9 8 7 6 5 4 3 2 1

Printed and bound in Italy

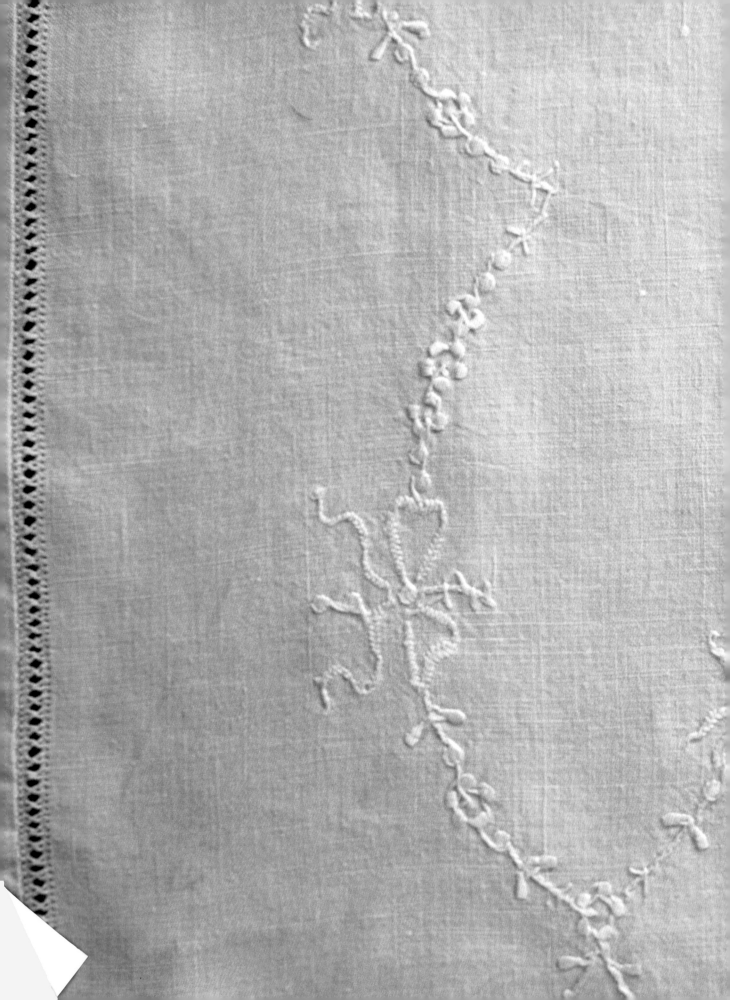